W9-BOB-071

The Holocaust and Other Genocides

DISCARD

The Holocaust and Other Genocides

An Introduction

Maria van Haperen
Wichert ten Have
Ben Kiernan
Martin Mennecke
Uğur Ümit Üngör
Ton Zwaan

Edited by
Barbara Boender
Wichert ten Have

NIOD Institute for War, Holocaust
and Genocide Studies
Amsterdam University Press

The publication of this book is made possible by a grant from
the Ministry of Health, Welfare and Sport.

Ministerie van Volksgezondheid,
Welzijn en Sport

www.holocoustandgenocide.nl

Editorial board:
Karen Polak (Anne Frank Foundation), Annemiek Gringold (Jewish Historical Museum), Dienke
Hondius (VU University Amsterdam), Maurice Kramer (Gymnasium Haganum), Maria van Haperen
(NIOD Institute voor War, Holocaust and Genocidestudies)

Cover design and lay-out: Gijs Mathijs Ontwerpers, Amsterdam
Maps: Bert Heesen Producties

ISBN   978 90 8964 381 0
e-ISBN   978 90 4851 528 8 (pdf)
NUR   689

© NIOD / Amsterdam University Press, Amsterdam 2012

All rights reserved. Without limiting the rights under copyright reserved above, no part of this
book may be reproduced, stored in or introduced into a retrieval system, or transmitted, in any
form or by any means (electronic, mechanical, photocopying, recording or otherwise) without
the written permission of both the copyright owner and the author of the book.

Every effort has been made to obtain permission to use all copyrighted illustrations reproduced in this book. Nonetheless, whosoever believes to have rights to this material is advised to
contact the publisher.

Contents

Introduction

The deliberate and systematic destruction of an entire people or ethnic group has been called the crime of all crimes. We are unable to comprehend rampant mass violence against a group of defenceless civilians solely aimed at annihilating them. Yet mass violence has always been a part of the history of mankind. The 20th and 21st centuries have even seen the worst episodes of mass violence, despite all pretensions of civilisation.

Conflict between and against ethnic groups has become a major part of political violence in the 20th century. Repeatedly, ethnic cleansing was used by states as a means to achieve national statehood and unity. Throughout history, religion has been an important motive in the killing of civilians. But the 19th century saw other factors, such as the merges of nations and class. Ideology turned out to be the force behind genocide. Bureaucratic efficiency, coupled with technological progress, shows us that violence can have disastrous, large-scale and irrevocable consequences.

1.   The Holocaust paradigm

The genocide of the Jews in Europe, known as the Holocaust, is a terrifying example of how mass violence can be used to exterminate an entire population. That, in effect, was the objective of the Holocaust: the mass murder of the Jews of Europe and the destruction of the Jewish people as a whole. The Holocaust provided the background to the Genocide Convention that was adopted by the member states of the United Nations on 9 December 1948. The term genocide was formulated by the Polish lawyer Raphael Lemkin, and his definition of genocide is used to this day.[1]

Research into other cases of genocide uses the Holocaust as a benchmark, whether consciously or subconsciously. This becomes evident in the methodology and the use of related terms such as 'victims', 'perpetrators' and 'bystanders'. When cases of mass violence and genocide are analysed or discussed, the Holocaust is often used as an example. This is known as the Holocaust paradigm.

2. Comparative research

This guidebook examines the Holocaust alongside a number of other genocides. Its primary aim is not to make a comparison in itself. However, analysing the similarities and differences can be a starting point for discussing how various cases of mass violence come about; about the fate of the victims, the background of the perpetrators and the involvement of witnesses to the mass murder. This analysis may reveal shared characteristics, such as ideology, a regime with revolutionary and utopian ambitions, internal division and circumstances of war.[2] At the same time, comparisons may reveal aspects of genocide that indicate significant differences. Differences might occur in the general context, the ideology and the political consequences, the international context and the nature of the conditions of war. Studying the Holocaust alongside other cases of genocide can help to clarify questions and suggest answers.

Every genocide has its own character and context. There are good reasons for being conscientious when comparing the Holocaust to other genocides. Generally speaking, processes of mass violence involve various phenomena in different contexts. The mass murders in Cambodia, those in Rwanda and the Holocaust were carried out under very different circumstances. Some researchers oppose to using the term genocide, as the general definition of genocide does not encompass all the complexities and differences. The definition does not, for example, include political killings of groups. Comparing cases of genocide can lead to simplification and can invoke unrealistic expectations.

Some researchers argue that other genocides cannot stand the comparison with the Holocaust. Firstly, because of the aforementioned differing circumstances of each of the genocides. Some scholars, such as historian Yehuda Bauer, accept the comparison but acknowledge the fact that the Holocaust was unparalleled in many ways. The Genocide Convention of 1948 mentions the intent to destroy a group in whole or in part. Bauer feels that here lies an essential difference. If the intention is to destroy every member of a group without exception, then that group ultimately has no chance of survival. Bauer and others consider this to be one of the decisive differences between the Holocaust and other cases of genocide. According to Bauer, it was the intention of the Nazis to wipe out all Jews, without exception. This is what made the Holocaust the most extreme form of genocide as well as a paradigm for every genocide, whenever and wherever it may occur.[3]

Bauer mentions some other aspects that are unique to the Holocaust, naming four of them in addition to the intent of destroying every single Jew. On the basis of these aspects Bauer refers to the Holocaust as a genocide 'without precedent':

1. The Germans killed Jews wherever they could: it was a universal genocide;
2. The core of National Socialist ideology was anti-Semitism, which was solely aimed against Jews;

3. The aim of National Socialism was a society based on a racial hierachy in which there was no place for the Jews;

4. The National Socialists wanted to destroy the roots of European civilisation. The Jews were perceived as a remnant of this, which is why they had to be destroyed.

Thus argued, some historians consider that treating the Holocaust within the general historical context of mass violence is 'diverting attention from what was unique about the annihilation of the Jews'. Others point to the danger that non-exclusive attention to the Holocaust may open the door to diminishment and possible denial. In some countries this could serve political goals. Diminishment of such severe crimes could stand in the way of people, perpetrators and bystanders alike, being held accountable for aiding and abetting in the persecution of the Jews.[4]

Yet there are important reasons for comparing the Holocaust to other genocides. For example, the term 'genocide' itself was conceived against the backdrop of the destruction of the Jews in Europe. Holocaust studies can be seen as the starting point for research into other genocides. Comparative studies allow us to make a distinction between the specific characteristics of the Holocaust and those of other cases of genocides. They also demonstrate how studying the Holocaust can help to provide insight into processes of genocide. Historian Ian Kershaw considers knowledge about the Third Reich to have taught an important lesson about the dark side of civilised society; how genocide can seem justifiable given the 'right' circumstances.

Simultaneously, knowledge about other genocides can provide new insights into aspects of the Holocaust. Historian Christopher Browning, for example, feels that the genocide in Rwanda sheds new light on perpetrator motives for genocide in general.[5]

3. Lessons from the past?

The Holocaust has become the paradigm in genocide studies. Historian Donald Bloxham argues that we can learn lessons from the past by comparing the Holocaust to other genocides. He is also keen to avoid creating a 'hierarchy' in which one genocide is seen as being 'worse' than another.

The millions of victims of genocidal violence in the 20th century are testimony to the ever present danger of genocide. There is good reason for taking the threat of genocide and mass violence seriously. Genocide prevention is an important issue. Great effort is being put into analysing cases of genocide and identifying common characteristics. These may be circumstances or events which, if detected at an early stage, could act as a warning of impending mass violence. Legal scholar Gregory Stanton identifies eight stages in the genocidal process: classification, symbolisation, dehumanisation, organisation, polarisation, preparation, extermination and denial. This supposition has given rise to research aimed at preventing genocide in the future, despite the awareness that any chances of successful prevention are small.[6]

4. Teaching about the Holocaust and other genocides

The Holocaust is vastly documented and knowledge is widely available — about the victims, the perpetrators and the bystanders; about the Third Reich and the ideology behind the mass destruction of the Jews; and also about the war that gave way to the genocidal process. Yet knowledge about other cases of mass violence and genocide especially tailored to secondary school education is far less easy to come by. News reports on ethnic violence or genocide denial give rise to questions among students and teachers. Those who are involved in secondary school education concerning the Holocaust will also want to refer to other cases of genocide.

Discussing the Holocaust might provoke many questions. How much did the victims know about what was going to happen to them? What led the perpetrators to their murderous behaviour? Would it have been possible to help the victims? How could a system come about that spawned such crimes? Could a catastrophe of this magnitude ever happen again? What are the implications of genocide denial? This book attempts to address these questions to their fullest extent.

A committee of international specialists in the field of Holocaust education compiled a report in which comparative studies between the Holocaust and other genocides are encouraged. At the same time, knowledge of modern genocides is often limited.[7] This book intends to provide basic, but fundamental, knowledge on genocide. Moreover, each of the articles refers to relevant and often in-depth literature on the subject. Teachers can use the conveniently arranged material in this textbook to answer questions along with their students and thus make an attempt to interpret both historical and present-day cases of genocide and mass violence.

All authors were asked to address certain issues and questions when asked which aspects of genocide should be covered when teaching the subject:

- What caused the genocide and what were the specific circumstances?
- How does a genocidal process develop once it has started? What factors play a role? What, for instance, is the role of ideology and propaganda in mobilising mass violence?
- How are genocides ended? What is the role of external powers and military intervention?
- What happens in a society in the aftermath of genocide? Is the genocide acknowledged? Is there any accountability? How are the victims treated? Is remembrance an important topic?
- Could genocide be prevented?[8]

The editors of this guidebook made a selection from various cases of genocide and mass violence. The first chapter provides a brief overview of the Holocaust which, in addition to providing an introduction to the subject, also serves as a benchmark for other genocides. The following chapter addresses the mass murder of the Armenians, on which the formulation of the concept of genocide was largely based. The subsequent chapters cover a number of cases of modern genocide: the former Yugoslavia, Rwanda and Cambodia. The chapter on the concept of genocide and developments in international law establishes a link between the various subjects. Additionally, a website has been developed to encourage further reading. On this website (www.holocaustandgenocide.nl) relevant articles are published, and all images are downloadable.

5. Task Force for Holocaust education

This guidebook was initiated during the 2011 Dutch chairmanship of the Task Force for International Cooperation on Holocaust Education, Remembrance and Research (ITF). The ITF, an intergovernmental body with the purpose of strengthening the memory of the Holocaust, now has 31 member states. The ITF — and this book — are anchored in the so-called Stockholm Declaration of 2000, in particular the following words:

'We must strengthen the moral commitment of our peoples, and the political commitment of our governments, to ensure that future generations can understand the causes of the Holocaust and reflect upon its consequences.' The declaration also speaks of the solemn responsibility to fight the evils of 'genocide, ethnic cleansing, racism, anti-Semitism and xenophobia'.[9]

In this spirit the Dutch chair added that 'the ITF should speak out on subjects such as the significance of the Holocaust and its relationship to other, more recent, genocides, as well as the different historical interpretations, and the mandate of the ITF regarding other groups of victims'.[10]

Under the auspices of the Dutch chair, both organisational and academic ambitions were addressed. On 27 and 28 November 2011, the Dutch delegation, operating on behalf of the Anne Frank Foundation, Herinneringscentrum Kamp Westerbork, the Hollandsche Schouwburg and the NIOD Institute for War, Holocaust and Genocide Studies, hosted the conference *The Holocaust and Other Genocides: Uses, Abuses and Misuses of the Holocaust Paradigm* in the Peace Palace in The Hague. Earlier that year, from 10 to 12 April, the expert meeting *Education on the Holocaust and Other Genocides* was held. The recommendations that were formulated during this meeting were used as the basis for this guidebook.[11]

The editorial board and several other advisors also made important contributions to this book. After establishing the authors' guidelines, the editorial board made invaluable comments on each chapter and on the book in general. Karen Polak of the Anne Frank Foundation and Annemiek Gringold of the Jewish Historical Museum applied themselves to this task with great enthusiasm. The suggestions made by Maurice Kramer (Gymnasium Haganum), Dienke Hondius (VU University Amsterdam) and Maria van Haperen (NIOD) — always referring to class-room practice — were invaluable. We are very grateful for the academic advice of

Johannes Houwink ten Cate, Vladimir Petrovic and Thijs Bouwknegt, all NIOD colleagues. And finally, Karin Dangermond (NIOD) and Inger Schaap (Anne Frank Foundation) contributed to the (photo) editing.

This textbook is made available to secondary school teachers in 31 countries, mostly within Europe. We hope that it will stimulate inspired teaching and well-grounded discussions on the Holocaust and other genocides.

Barbara Boender
Wichert ten Have

NIOD Institute for War, Holocaust and Genocide Studies

Notes

1   The UN Genocide Convention on the Prevention and Punishment of the Crime of Genocide, adopted by the UN General Assembly on 9 December 1948, http://www.un.org/millennium/law/iv-1.htm.

2   Eric D. Weitz 2003, *A Century of Genocide. Utopias of Race and Nations*. Oxford, p. 15.

3   Yehuda Bauer, On the Holocaust and Other Genocides. Joseph and Rebecca Meyerhoff Annual Lecture, 5 October 2006. First Printing, February 2007.

4   Review Forum Donald Bloxham, *Journal of Genocide Research*, Vol. 13, 1-2, March- January 2011, pp. 144-146. See Omar Bartov, Doris Bergen 2011, *Paper on the Holocaust and Other Genocides*, ITF Education Working Group.

5   Christopher R. Browning, Revisiting the Holocaust Perpetrators. 'Why Did They Kill?' *Nooit Meer Auschwitz Lezing*, Amsterdam, 27 January 2011, p. 23; I. Kershaw, 'Normality' and Genocide: The Problem of Historicization' in: Ian Kershaw 2008, *Hitler, the Germans and the Final Solution*. London.

6   Report Stockholm International Forum 2004: Preventing Genocide. Stockholm 2004; Barbara Harff, 'No Lessons Learned from the Holocaust? Assessing Risks of Genocide and Political Mass Murder since 1955. *American Political Science Review*, Vol. 97, nr. 1. February 2003, pp. 57-73.

7   *The Holocaust and other genocides*, ITF, December 2010, http://www.holocausttaskforce.org/images/itf_data/EWG_Holocaust_and_Other_Genocides_copy.pdf

8   As stated by Ton Zwaan, Report of the Expert Meeting on Education on the Holocaust and Other Genocides.

9   Declaration of the Stockholm International Forum on the Holocaust, January 2000.

10 Declaration of the Chair, Ambassador Karel de Beer, March 2011.

11 Report of the Expert Meeting on Education on the Holocaust and Other Genocides, 10-12 April 2011. Amsterdam, June 2011.

The Holocaust, 1933-1941-1945

Wichert ten Have and Maria van Haperen

'Early in the morning of 1 June 1943, the names of those who were to depart for the east in the waiting freight train were read aloud in the deadly silence of the barracks. [...] We tried to boost each other's morale. We are heading for the east, probably Poland. Perhaps we will meet family members there and friends who have already left. We will have to work hard and will suffer great deprivation. The summers will be hot and the winters freezing cold. But our spirits are high. We will not allow anyone or anything to dampen our spirits. [...] Of course, none of us knew exactly what was ahaid of us. We had to make the best of it. We would do what we could to stay together and to survive the war. It was the only sensible thing you could say to each other in such circumstances. [...] After our carriage had been packed with as many people as possible and the door locked from the outside with massive hooks, De Vries did a headcount: there were 62 of us, plus a pram. With all of our baggage, we were like herrings packed in a barrel. There was barely any room to stretch your legs. [...] The first problem we tried to solve was that of deciding on the best position to make the journey, sitting or standing. There was no obvious answer that applied as a general rule. Some could sit as long as there were others who stood. The pram and the barrels also took up a lot of room. Even before the train left, the barrel was being put to use because many were unable to control their nerves. It was agreed that two women would take turns to hold up a coat when one of their fellow gender needed to use the barrel. Of course, the same applied for the men. As you can imagine, the stench in the carriage soon became unbearable.'[1]

Jules Schelvis (b. 1921), survivor of the Holocaust from the Netherlands

Introduction

During World War II, approximately 5.7 million Jews were murdered by Nazi Germany. The dead were not victims of war, but they were killed because they were Jewish.

The Holocaust developed in stages, but its broad outlines were clear from the start. In the first phase of the war, 'racially alien elements', primarily Jews, but also Roma and Sinti, were to be purged from German territories. There were mass executions, starting from the invasion of Poland on 1 September 1939, but they intensified after the attack on the Soviet Union on 22 June 1941. By late 1941, there was a policy to deport the Jews and ultimately murder all of them.

This happened mainly by suffocating the victims on an industrial scale in specially designed camps with gas chambers and crematoria. All of this called for a massive logistic operation, which was carefully prepared and carried out, not only by special officers but also by officials from the regular services, such as the railways. These factors make the extermination of the Jews a genocide without a precedent.

Holocaust

Over the years, the murder of European Jews has been given various different names. After World War II, very little was generally said in public about the atrocities. Raoul Hilberg, pioneering historian of the Holocaust, spoke of the 'destruction of the Jews'. The well-known television series *The Holocaust* (1978) brought the persecution and ultimate murder of European Jews to wider public attention. The concept of 'Holocaust' (from the ancient Greek 'sacrifice by fire') had already been in existence, but would now be used internationally to describe the tragedy of the murder of the Jews. This is reflected in the name for Holocaust Memorial Day on 27 January, the date designated by the United Nations to commemorate the murder of the Jews. The name is also used as a title for many museums and centres devoted to the subject. Others, and especially Jews themselves, prefer to use the term 'Shoah', the Hebrew word for catastrophe.

Some historians consider the persecution in the 1930s to be an integral part of the Holocaust. Others argue that the Holocaust started in the autumn of 1941, when Nazi Germany began to organise and carry out the mass extermination of the Jews. Primarily because of the anti-Semitism involved, some people use the term Holocaust specifically to describe the extermination of the Jews. Others argue that other persecuted groups, such as the Roma, should also be considered victims of the Holocaust.

---

1. Historical background

The persecution of the Jews did not take place in isolation. The Holocaust must be placed in the wider context of World War II and associated violence, such as the murder of millions of Polish and Russian prisoners of war. The area of Eastern Europe and the west of the Soviet Union was the scene of mass violence of many different kinds.

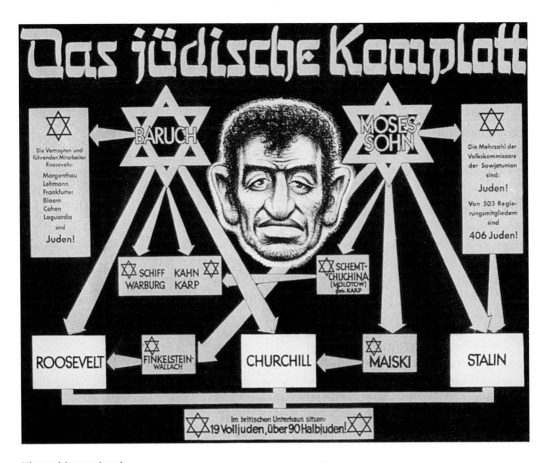

'The Jewish conspiracy'
Source: Beeldbank WO2 — NIOD

The Holocaust would have been unthinkable without anti-Semitism, a deep-rooted hatred of Jews. This hatred originated from early Christianity. The myth that the Jews were guilty of Christ's death was particularly persistent. Jews were also accused of the ritual murder of Christians. In times of disasters, such as plagues, Jews served as scapegoats. As a result of negative stereotyping, Jews were excluded from many professions and forced into exile or even tortured and killed in pogroms.

After the French Revolution, Jews in Western and Central Europe were accorded equal rights. However, after the 19th century, Jews were also deemed to be responsible for the negative consequences of industrialisation and individualisation. Jews were blamed for instigating capitalism for their own gain. Similar accusations were made about socialism. Developments in science brought about ideas on race and evolution that fostered the emergence of a new racial anti-Semitism. According to this race theory, Jews were 'alien to the people' and deemed to be a 'problem'. The term 'Jewish question' (*Judenfrage*) had originally been used in the context of a debate about the emancipation of the Jews. But now, this 'inferior race' was a 'problem' for which radical anti-Semites believed a solution had to be found.

Anti-Semitism

Anti-Semitism was an international phenomenon. After World War I in Germany, anti-Semitism became part of the prevailing sense of dissatisfaction. The wounded sense of national pride went hand-in-hand with distaste for the new, democratic Weimar Republic and a yearning for a strong, authoritarian state. This growing nationalism became a breeding ground for anti-Semitism in Germany, which enabled National Socialism to flourish. The human ideal was 'Aryan', which meant blond hair, blue eyes and 'Germanic' blood. There was no room for other 'races', for the disabled or those deemed antisocial.

Since their rise to power in 1933, the Nazi party had fiercely suppressed their political opponents. Discrimination and persecution of Jews and Roma also began to take hold. This policy became enshrined in racist legislation. The Jews, who until then had often considered themselves to be completely German, became isolated and were deprived of their rights. The Nuremberg Laws of 1935 prohibited relationships and marriages between 'racially pure Germans' and others. During the pogrom on 9 and 10 November 1938, this anti-Semitism broke out into violence. On *Kristallnacht*, the windows of Jewish shops were smashed and Jewish property stolen. But that was not all: on that night, many Jews were also attacked and even murdered. Jews were arrested to encourage others to emigrate. Even before the war, it was clear to the Nazis that there would be no room for the Jews in the Germany they envisioned.

2. World War II

During the 1930s, tens of thousands of Jews emigrated from Germany and Austria, leaving behind most of their possessions. There had long been ideas about enforced emigration, including a plan to send the Jews to Madagascar. National Socialists at all levels were accustomed to the use of violence in anti-Semitic operations.

In the autumn of 1939, Germany conquered Poland. As the German army advanced to the east, a wave of mass murders began. According to the plan, these were targeted at the Polish elite: intellectuals, priests, officers and political leaders. In the secret part of the pact between the Soviet Union and Nazi Germany, known as the Molotov-Ribbentrop Pact, Poland was divided in two, with one part under the Soviet and one under the German sphere of influence. Central and Western Poland became part of the German Reich, with the central section being renamed Wartheland. What remained, including the cities of Warsaw, Lviv and Kraków, was ruled as a protectorate under the name Generalgovernment. The plan was for Poland to be prepared for habitation and exploitation by Germans. The Slav people were considered to be inferior and at best to be used for slave labour. Space, or *Lebensraum*, was to be created through the forced migration of hundreds of thousands of Poles from west to east, including many Jews. Two million Jews came under Nazi control as a result of the victory over Poland. After the military campaign, special units were sent into the country to fight 'enemies of the Reich'. As well as the Polish elite, many Jews also fell victim. Thousands of them died at the end of 1939. A plan had now been drawn up to deport all Jews to some kind of reservation on the eastern border of German-occupied Poland. In the autumn of 1939, Polish and Austrian Jews were already being deported. In 1940, the deportations temporarily stopped because the General Government faced problems accommodating all of the Jews there. Throughout these operations, countless Jews were murdered by the SS and the police.

2.1   The isolation of the Jews

The German authorities had now begun to establish ghettos. Bringing Jews together would make deportation at a later stage easier. Until then, the Jews had to carry out forced labour. In February 1940 a ghetto was established in the industrial city of Lódz that would serve as a model ghetto for the Germans.

These ghettos were soon overpopulated and had few amenities. Forced labour was part of life in a ghetto. The Germans appointed representatives of the Jewish population, who would be responsible for organising internal governance as the Jewish Council (*Judenrat*), but who

Jews flee from a town in Lithuania, 1939.
Source: Beeldbank WO2 — NIOD

were otherwise completely dependent on the Germans. Conditions in the ghettos such as Lódz, Warsaw, Lublin and many others varied, but were usually terrible.

Since early 1940, Norway, Denmark, the Netherlands, Belgium and France had all been occupied by Germany. Here too, the Jews were deprived of their civil rights, and were persecuted like the Jews in Germany. Across the occupied and captured territories, Jews were forced into ghettos or deported to the Polish region around Lublin. In the meantime, mentally handicapped people from Germany and elsewhere had been transferred to special institutions, where they became victims of the euthanasia programme on Hitler's orders.

Aktion T4 – Euthanasia programme

From the end of the 1930s, Hitler ordered a programme of euthanasia to be carried out on people who were deemed 'unworthy' to live, referring to the disabled and the mentally or incurably ill. From 1940, gassing experiments were conducted within this programme. The *Aktion T4* doctors developed a method which could be used to gas 20 patients at the same time. Following church protests, the programme was abandoned, but not before 360,000 people had been killed. The *Aktion T4* experiences proved very useful in the destruction of the Jewish population. This operation took its name from the headquarters of the Nazi euthanasia programme, which was based in Tiergartenstrasse 4, in Berlin.

All the necessary conditions for genocide were in place by the spring of 1941. Thousands of Jews had already been deported and murdered. Those who remained were isolated from the rest of society, forced to live in unhygienic conditions and desperately short of food.

3.   After the invasion of Russia

On 22 June 1941, German troops invaded the Soviet Union in what was known as Operation Barbarossa. They expected to vanquish the Red Army within a few months. As soon as the first territories were conquered, there were systematic mass murders of Jews. An order had been issued for all communists captured to be killed. Special units, known as *Einsatzgruppen*, followed the front line to see off potential enemies. They were supported by police and *Wehrmacht* units. Partisans were executed. The *Einsatzgruppen* soon turned to the Jews, and executed hundreds of thousands of them.

3.1   War of annihilation

In the months before the attack on the Soviet Union, Hitler had informed his most important generals of his war plans. He warned that this would not be a conventional war, 'but a *war of annihilation*'.[2]

According to Hitler, it was imperative that the attack on Russia achieved a military conquest which would enable the Third Reich to last for 1000 years. In his view, Russia had the inex-

Jews in Krakau, Poland, 1940
Source: Beeldbank WO2 — NIOD

haustible economic reserves and the *Lebensraum* the German people needed. A war against Bolsheviks and Jews could therefore be very little else than a war of annihilation. They were the sworn enemies of National Socialism.

20-8-1941

'[...] We talk about the Jewish question. The *Führer* believes that his prophecy in the *Reichstag* has been confirmed: if the Jews were successful in provoking another world war, this war would lead to their own annihilation. With almost unnerving accuracy, this prophecy is being confirmed in these weeks and months. In the east, the Jews must now pay the price [...] Jewry is a foreign body among civilised peoples and their behaviour in the last 30 years has been so devastating that the response of these peoples is completely understandable, necessary, and yes, even completely natural. In any case, in the world to come, the Jews will not have much to laugh about. In Europe, there is already a united front against Jewry.'[3]

Diary entry by Joseph Goebbels

The Germans were supported by anti-Communist militias from Ukraine, Lithuania and elsewhere. Most of the population was anti-Russian and anti-Communist. There often was a deep-rooted anti-Semitism among the population. After two decades of independence, the Baltic countries were again occupied by the Russians in June 1940. Large groups of the population were deported. Many Baltic and Ukrainian nationalists blamed the Jews for this and welcomed the arrival of the German troops.

Until the autumn of 1941, the mass slaughter of the Jews spread. Women and children now fell victim as well. This more radical approach was encouraged by Heinrich Himmler, *Reichsführer* of the SS, and Reinhard Heydrich, head of the Security Police and Security Service (SiPo and SD). In Latvia and Lithuania, men were ordered to carry out forced labour. Women and children were systematically murdered. In rural areas, many Jews, including the men, were murdered with the help of local anti-Communist militia. On 7 and 8 December 1941, there was a notorious series of murders in which 20,000 Jews were killed. Outside Vilnius in Lithuania, in the Ponary Forest, there were regular mass executions between July 1941 and July 1944. Local people were often encouraged by the Germans to take part in the murdering.

In Ukraine in the summer of 1941, SS units and the police began to murder Jewish women and children as well as men. The Jews were collected in the cities. The Jewish men were forced to dig pits and trenches just outside the city. All victims were marched to the place of execution, where they were shot row by row. This pattern was repeated in many places.

When the capital Kiev was captured, all the Jews in the city were ordered to assemble. On 29 and 30 September 1941, 33,771 Jews were shot dead on the edge of a ravine in Babi Yar outside the city. Afterwards, the edges were blown up to cover the bodies with earth. In Belarus, a second series of murders followed some months later, killing tens of thousands of Jews.

Many hundreds of thousands of Jews were murdered in the areas of the Soviet Union captured by the Germans. It was almost impossible to escape these deadly campaigns. Some Jews survived by fleeing further eastwards, to the areas still held by the Soviets. However, the persecution of the Jews was not limited to Poland and the former Soviet Union territories. In Serbia, there had been a German military administration since the spring of 1941, supported by a regime of collaborators. Thousands of Jews, including women and children, were 'brought to justice'. In Romania, it was the country's own military and police units that deported the Jews and Roma. Sometimes, the executions took place in Romania itself. In Odessa, there was a mass execution ordered by Romanian dictator Ion Antonescu, killing around 25,000 Jews.

4. The final solution

In August and September 1941, the German advance into the Soviet Union stagnated. The Red Army was offering resistance. In late 1941, Germany began the deportation of Jews to Poland. It had now become clear that the developments in the war would prevent the Jews from being driven further to the east.

'[...] After the Germans came, we did not know what to do, it was appalling.

Eventually, we were told we were to be deported. We were allowed to take 20 kg of luggage and fifty zloty per person. They locked up half of the town. They sent the rest to Izbica and Wieprz. The people transported included both poor and rich Jews.

[...] On arrival in Izbica, everyone was allocated a dwelling. Usually, three families had to share one house. If you were lucky, there were just two families in one house. But some people had to share a house with four families, which was extremely cramped.

[...] It was not long before we heard that more were arriving from Kulice. This made it extremely cramped in the ghetto. It was a really small town, where around 200 Jews had lived before the war. The synagogue was in the middle. Space was so limited, that Jews had to live on the gallery in the synagogue. And then there were transports from Czechoslovakia and from Berlin. People began to sell their possessions, because they had no income. You were not allowed out, at five o'clock everything was locked.

The Jewish Council also ensured that people went to work. But because they were beaten, people no longer wanted to work. So people who had nothing left, and no longer knew what to do, would suggest: "If you give me five zloty, I will work for you." I had to live on something and had no choice. I had my family to care for.'[4]

Chaskiel Menche (1910-1984), survivor of Sobibor

The ghettos in the German-controlled areas were overpopulated and unable to accommodate Jews deported from the West. Attempts were made to find more radical and definitive solutions. The local initiatives reflected the wishes of Berlin. In Chelmno, Western Poland, an extermination camp was established, intended solely to kill people. More than 150,000 Jews and Roma would be murdered in this camp in the period up to 1943. Previous experience acquired with the disabled in the *Aktion T4* programme was deployed. The victims were now driven into freight trucks. The exhaust gases from the engines in the sealed freight trucks suffocated them within twenty minutes.

These were the first steps in the final solution, the *Endlösung*, as the Nazi leaders envisaged it. On 12 December 1941, Hitler addressed the meeting of party managers on the 'Jewish question'.[5] As Goebbels noted in his diary, Hitler argued that he wanted a final solution to the problem. He had warned the Jews that if they were to cause another world war, they would thereby bring about their own annihilation. As the Second World War was now a fact, the annihilation of the Jewish people should be the result, according to Hitler's logic.

Hitler and the extermination of the Jews

The personal role of Hitler in the Holocaust has long been a subject for discussion among historians. Was the annihilation of the Jews part of a plan he had long prepared? Or was it something that gradually became a reality, as a result of the actions of national and local Nazi officers? There is no doubt that the realisation of Hitler's idea of annihilating the Jews was influenced by circumstances. In September or October 1941, the decision to murder all Jews must have been taken at the highest level, in line with Hitler's views; and carried out by Nazi officers who took action that reflected the *Führer's* views. This would have been unthinkable without widespread, murderous anti-Semitism.

Heinrich Himmler took responsibility for overall supervision of the *Endlösung*. Reinhard Heydrich was given the task of coordinating implementation. The SS officer and *Regierungsrat* Adolph Eichmann, head of subdepartment IV B 4 of the *Reichssicherheitshauptamt* (Main Security Office, RSHA), was responsible for the organisation of the deportation of the Jews outside of the Reich and the Soviet Union.

On 20 January 1942, the Wannsee Conference was held in Berlin, where Heydrich informed leading officials from ministries and administrative bodies in the East about the policy against the Jews. The minutes still referred to *Endlösung* and labour. In reality, those present were told about the necessity to collaborate in the murder of all European Jews. Heydrich, assisted by Eichmann, spoke of the need to eradicate the Jews. For example, they would gradually be driven in colonies towards the east, constructing roads as they progressed. Many would die in the process. Any survivors were to be dealt with accordingly. In this context, 'practical experience... [was] already being collected which is of the greatest importance in relation to the future final solution of the Jewish question'. This was a reference to the methods of extermination to be used later, such as gassing.

4.1   Aktion Reinhardt

From October 1941, preparations were made in the General Government for the mass extermination of the Jews. There were already executions in numerous places. Officials from the west who were experienced with the 'euthanasia programme' were transferred to Lublin. This experience was to be used in Poland. It became clear that the new campaigns to exterminate Jews were primarily to be organised within the General Government. Starting in March 1942, the SS and the police cleared the ghettos.

On 27 March 1942, Heydrich fell victim to an attack by the Czech resistance. From then on, the General Government operation was known as *Aktion Reinhardt*, or Operation Reinhardt. Aktion Reinhardt was under the central control of SS officer Odilo Globocnik. Jews were now being hunted down across the whole area. On the orders of Himmler, any men fit for work were put in camps. The remaining Jews were assembled and murdered on the spot or deported. The final destination of these deportations was the extermination camps of Aktion Reinhardt. Only death awaited there.

'We were taken away in 1943. Early in the morning, at around five o'clock, we were woken by shots. SS officers forced their way into our houses and marched all the Jews to the market square. At first, we hoped they would take us to a labour camp.

We had heard about Sobibor. After being transported, we found ourselves opposite a large gate. I remember that it was only marked *SS-Sonderkommando*. This was Sobibor. Then the gate was opened and we went in. I could not believe that this was an extermination camp, because it looked so nice. It was 23 April 1943. The sun was shining and it seemed like a beautiful summer's day. I knew we were going to die, but, at the same time, I could not believe it. It was just so beautiful there. When people had talked about an extermination camp, I had imagined a dangerous place, something that the Jews called *gehennen*, like hell. In those kinds of places, people are dirty and roam around and you can see fire everywhere. But here I saw a beautiful village, with a nice little station, although I could see fire two hundred metres ahead. I realised that this was the end.

Suddenly I heard a voice that said: "Men to the right, women and children to the left." I was standing next to my mother, my younger brother was next to my father. I was fifteen. I'm still not tall, but then I was small and thin. I thought I had no chance of survival.'[6]

Thomas Blatt (b. 1927), Sobibor survivor

In addition to the existing camp in Chelmno, three special extermination camps were established: Belzec (March 1942), in the east of Poland, for the extermination of Jews from Lublin and Lviv and the surrounding area; Sobibor (May 1942), also in the east, for the gassing of Dutch, French and Polish Jews; and Treblinka (July 1942), north-east of Warsaw, intended for the extermination of Jews from the Warsaw ghetto and across Poland. When the gas chambers and crematoria had been completed, this would mean death by suffocation. The murders reached their climax between July and November 1942. Hundreds of thousands of people were sent to the extermination camps by train. During this period, more than two million Jews were killed in the gas chambers.

Aktion Reinhardt
Estimated number of deaths[7]:

Belzec	435,000
Sobibor	170,000
Treblinka	850,000

4.2   Auschwitz

Chelmno and the Majdanek concentration camp, built alongside Polish Lublin, were also used as extermination camps after 1942, as was Auschwitz. Starting in May 1940, the former complex of barracks at Auschwitz was adapted for the imprisonment of Polish opponents of the Nazi regime. Later, there were other nationalities, prisoners of war, political and ideological opponents of the Nazis, resistance fighters who had been captured and the disabled. In March 1941, construction started on Birkenau, a few kilometres from Auschwitz. In September 1941, the first experiments with the deadly gas Zyklon-B were conducted in the crematoria.

Birkenau was taken into use in the spring of 1942. By this time, Auschwitz was also operating as an extermination camp. The first trains packed with Jews started to arrive in March 1942. At the end of 1942, the first groups of Sinti and Roma were being deported to Birkenau. Unlike in the 'Aktion Reinhardt' camps, there was a selection on arrival: deportees who were capable of working were separated from those sent straight to the gas chambers. Initially, the gas chambers were improvised bunkers, but in 1944 new gas chambers began to be used in Birkenau. The train line was extended right into the camp, so that thousands of people could be exterminated every day. With the arrival of the Hungarian Jews in May 1944, the extermination of the Jews in Auschwitz-Birkenau reached its climax. This mass murder on an industrial scale of more than one million people made Auschwitz a symbol of the extermination of the Jews.[8]

> **Auschwitz as a symbol of the Holocaust**
>
> Auschwitz-Birkenau, Monowitz and the approximately 40 other neighbouring camps became the largest complex of concentration and extermination camps.
>
> On 27 January 1945, an advance guard of Red Army troops freed the 7,000 prisoners who remained in the camp. Approximately 1.3 million people were murdered in Auschwitz. In the 1990s, 27 January was declared as International Holocaust Memorial Day by the United Nations .

5. Persecution of the Jews in other countries

Allies of Nazi Germany also persecuted Jews, sometimes on their own initiative, sometimes under German pressure. In Croatia, Slovakia and Romania, countless Jews died as a result of persecution. Bulgaria, however, refused to surrender its own Jews. Finland also successfully resisted the German policy of persecution. In the non-occupied part of France, the Vichy regime surrendered only foreign Jews.

In the occupied areas, the local authorities also had to deal with the Nazi policy of persecution. The German occupying authorities pushed hard for the deportation of the Jews. Following the deportation of foreign Jews from occupied France on 26 March 1942, the yellow star badge was introduced as a recognisable symbol, marking the start of the systematic persecution of all Jews. The same happened in the Netherlands and Belgium. There was a continuous stream of trains departing from the Netherlands, with the assistance of the local authorities, deporting people not only to Auschwitz, but also to Sobibor. This meant that the percentage of Jews who survived the war in the Netherlands was extremely low in relative terms.

Denmark enjoyed semi-independent status thanks to a treaty with Germany. When the Ger-

Gas chamber in Auschwitz
Source: Beeldbank WO2 — NIOD

mans began to persecute the Jewish population here too, the resistance succeeded in evacuating 7,000 (of 8,000 in total) Jews safely to Sweden. Other Danish Jews were deported to the Theresienstadt camp, just one of the stop-off points en route to the extermination camps.

In Greece, Jews were systematically persecuted. Starting in March 1943, the large Jewish community from Thessaloniki was transported to Auschwitz.

In Italy, Mussolini's Fascist regime gradually introduced anti-Semitic legislation. After occupation by Nazi Germany, the systematic persecution of the Jews became an everyday reality.

In Hungary, Jews were persecuted and imprisoned by Hungarian right-wing militia. However, the regime itself did not hand over the Jews to the Germans. But after the occupation by Nazi Germany in March 1944, 437,000 Hungarian Jews were transported to Auschwitz, where most of them were murdered.

5.1   The Holocaust in Eastern and Western Europe

The position and the experience of the Holocaust victims — the Jews, but also the Roma and Sinti — in different parts of Europe often varied greatly.

The Jews in Germany had been subjected to persecution since 1933. Tens of thousands of them had emigrated, and the Jews who remained behind were at the mercy of the Nazi terror.

In the occupied areas of Poland, the Baltic countries and the western Soviet Union, Jews were shot by the ten thousand or hundred thousand in mass executions, often in their home town, village or region. From 1942 onwards millions of Jews were sent to death camps where they were exterminated. The violence was also directed against other citizens and against prisoners of war from the Soviet Union. These areas in Eastern Europe have been referred to as 'bloodlands' (Timothy Snyder) and described as 'extremely violent societies' (Christian Gerlach).

In Western Europe the Jews were often part of a small minority. The German occupation regimes initially created the impression that they wanted to implement a moderate policy towards the Jews. The National Socialists viewed the Northern Europeans as racially related. Anti-Jewish measures were implemented gradually. Despite the processes of identification, isolation, expropriation and deportation, the chances of survival for Jews in Western Europe were higher than in the East. The large majority of Jews who were deported to Poland were exterminated in the death camps.

The Jews who remained in Western Europe had two important means of survival: in some cases they were able to flee to a neutral country such as Switzerland or Sweden; others escaped the violence by going into hiding. There were also Jews who in some way or other managed to conceal the fact that they were Jewish. In all of these cases they were forced to rely on help from others.

The fate of the Jews varied per country. In fascist Italy, anti-Semitism was not at the heart of the ideology of the regime although anti-Semitic legislation did come into effect in 1938. Italy was relatively safe for Jews, even those who had fled from German-occupied France. France in 1940 was home to some 300,000 to 320,000 Jews, most of whom did not have French nationality, or had only recently acquired it. In Belgium there were around 55,600 Jews, 95% of whom were non-Belgian. Denmark and Norway had few refugees; the total number of Jews in these countries was 8,000 and 2,000 respectively, making up 0.18 % of the population of Denmark and 0.05 % of the population of Norway.

A large proportion of Dutch Jews did not survive the persecution.

The situation in the Netherlands was almost the opposite. There were around 118,000 Dutch Jews as well as almost 22,000 Jewish refugees from Germany and Austria. The proportion of Jews deported from the Netherlands and murdered was exceptionally high: 75 %. In Belgium this was 40 % and in France 25 %. There is no single explanation for this high percentage in the Netherlands. People have pointed to the level of integration of Dutch Jews and the geographical limitations to resistance as well as to the cooperation with the German occupiers by the Dutch authorities and the nature of the occupying regime.

Deportationtrain France
Bron: Beeldbank WO2 — NIOD

6. The victims

'Our language lacks words to describe this offence [...]'[9]
Primo Levi, writer and camp survivor

Writing about the fate of the victims can never do justice to the suffering they faced. The testimony of survivors is an important source of information on the experiences of the Holocaust victims.

Around 1942, most Jews in Poland and Eastern Europe lived in ghettos or in isolated parts of cities and villages. Their living conditions had worsened horribly: many, including numerous children and elderly, died of starvation and exhaustion. In the major persecution and extermination operations of 1942, the situation deteriorated: the SS and police dragged people from their homes. The disabled and children were often shot on the spot. Attempts to escape or

Zentralstelle für jüdische
Auswanderung Amsterdam
Adama v. Scheltemaplein 1
Telefoon 97001

1

N⁰ 27525

OPROEPING!

Aan ▓▓▓▓▓▓▓▓▓▓▓   L   185   No. 9

Cypresstr 82   Den Haag.

U moet zich voor eventueele deelname aan een, onder politietoezichtstaande, werk-verruiming in Duitschland voor persoonsonderzoek en geneeskundige keuring naar het door-gangskamp Westerbork, station Hooghalen, begeven.

18 AUG. 1942   — 1.00

Daartoe moet U op .... óm .... uur

op de verzamelplaats DEN HAAG STAATSSPOOR — ZIE BIJLAGE .... aanwezig zijn

Als bagage mag medegenomen worden:

1 **koffer of rugzak**
1 **paar werklaarzen**
2 **paar sokken**
2 **onderbroeken**
2 **hemden**
1 **werkpak**
2 **wollen dekens**
2 **stel beddengoed (overtrek met laken)**
1 **eetnap**
1 **drinkbeker**
1 **lepel en**
1 **pullover**
handdoek en toiletartikelen

en eveneens marschproviand voor 3 dagen en de voor die tijd geldige distributiekaarten.
De mee te nemen bagage moet in gedeelten gepakt worden.

a. **Noodzakelijke reisbehoeften**
daartoe behooren: 2 dekens, 1 stel beddegoed, levensmiddelen voor 3 dagen, toiletgerei, etensbord, eetbestek, drinkbeker,

b. **Groote bagage**
De onder b. vermelde bagage moet worden gepakt in een stevige koffer of rugzak, welke op duidelijke wijze voorzien moet zijn van **naam, voornamen, geboortedatum en het woord „Holland".**
Gezinsbagage is niet toegestaan.
Het voorgaande moet nauwkeurig in acht genomen worden, daar de groote bagage in de plaats van vertrek afzonderlijk ingeladen wordt.
De verschillende bewijs- en persoonspapieren mogen **niet bij de bagage verpakt worden**, doch moeten, voor onmiddellijk vertoon gereed, medegedragen worden.
De woning moet ordelijk achtergelaten en afgesloten worden, de huissleutels moeten worden medegenomen.
Niet medegenomen mogen worden: levend huisraad.

K 372

Call for Westerbork transit camp, the Netherlands
Source: Beeldbank WO2—NIOD

Deportation from Amsterdam, the Netherlands, 20 June 1943
Source: Beeldbank WO2 — NIOD

signs of disobedience were met with gunfire. Sometimes there was a selection process after which Jews who were capable of working for the Germans could remain with their families: they had no choice but to stand by and watch as others were taken away. In Eastern Poland, they were mainly shot dead outside the towns and cities. In the west, the Jews were assembled in stations and deported in miserable conditions, without facilities, in overfull freight trains to the extermination camps. In the camp, they were removed from the trains by Trawniki workers, who often originated from Ukraine. Some of them former prisoners of war, they had been trained in camp Trawniki. Everything was then removed from the victims: possessions, jewellery, money and clothing. Their hair was shaved off. Often the Jews were told that they were going to shower, to disinfect them. Then they were led into the gas chambers. Some Jews were selected to work in *Sonderkommandos* in the gas chambers. They were forced to remove the bodies from the gas chambers, take any gold and silver from the teeth and carry away the corpses. Initially, they were thrown into mass graves, but when these were full, the bodies were incinerated in crematoria. Here too, the hard work was left to the Jewish *Sonderkommandos*.

'Der Ewige Jude'
Source: Beeldbank WO2 — NIOD

> **Roma and Sinti**
>
> Roma and Sinti, sometimes referred to by others as gypsies, had been victims of discrimination and persecution for centuries. When the National Socialists came to power in Germany in 1933, this persecution intensified. Like the Jews, they were seen as a threat to society. Roma and Sinti were incarcerated in camps and were often sterilised. Like the Jewish population, Roma and Sinti were also deported by train to camps in Eastern Europe. In Auschwitz-Birkenau, a special 'Gypsy camp' was established, in which all residents were murdered in August 1944. Estimates vary on the exact total number of victims. They range from 100,000 to 300,000.

6.1 Jewish and other resistance

In the spring of 1942 it became clear that the Germans intended to clear the ghettos. The chairman of the Jewish Council in the Warsaw ghetto, Adam Czerniakov, was ordered to designate 5,000 Jews to be deported every day. Aware of their fate and unable to prevent it, Czerniakov committed suicide. Almost daily, residents from the ghetto were taken by train to the extermination camp Treblinka. In early September 1942, the Germans assembled all the Jews who were not fit for work. In just a few weeks, more than 250,000 people, including nearly all children, were taken away and murdered.

In 1943, the remaining Jews in the east were taken to concentration camps. When it became clear that even the Jews who had stayed in the ghetto were to be deported, a desperate, but fierce resistance ensued. In the fighting that followed, thousands of Jewish fighters were killed. There were also uprisings in other places, for example in the Bialystok ghetto and even in the Treblinka and Sobibor extermination camps. In Sobibor, a number of prisoners succeeded in escaping and joined the resistance.

Jews also resisted persecution in other ways. Many attempted to flee, to hide or take refuge, with the support of local people willing to help. Others took part in resistance activities or joined the partisans. However, resistance and uprisings often resulted in reprisals. In these revenge operations, many innocent people were killed by the Germans, all civilians, among them many Jews. During *Aktion Erntefest* in November 1943, the SS and police units shot dead 42,000 Jews from various camps in just a few days. Some of the Jews who were fit for work were brought together in the remaining concentration camps.

6.2   International responses

There was hardly any help for the Jews. There were occasional cases of ingenious interventions. A well-known example is that of the Swedish diplomat Raoul Wallenberg, who saved thousands of Jews in Budapest by issuing them with Swedish passports. Despite this and other individual actions, it was not possible to prevent the genocide. Sparse but accurate reports about the mass murders gradually filtered through to the Allies. One example came from SS officer Kurt Gerstein, who took the risk of informing the outside world about what was happening in Belzec.

'[...] A few minutes later a train arrived from Lviv, with 45 carriages holding 6,000 people, of whom 1,450 were already dead on arrival. Behind the small, barbed wire window, terrified children, young people, men and women. The train pulled in and 200 Ukrainians, equipped for the task, opened the doors and lashed the people with their whips. The Jews crept out of the cars.

A loudspeaker issued instructions: to remove all clothing, even artificial limbs and glasses. A young Jewish boy handed out pieces of string for people to tie their shoes together. All valuables and money had to be handed in at the ticket window marked Valuables, no tickets or receipts were issued. Women and girls were to have their hair cut off in the Barber's barracks.

[...] They gradually came closer to the place where I was standing with Wirth, in front of the gas chambers. Men, women, young girls, children, babies, cripples, all of them completely naked, walking past in a row. On the corner, a sturdy SS officer stood, with a loud

Cleaning out the Warsaw Ghetto, 1943
Source: Beeldbank WO2 — NIOD

unctuous voice. "Nothing will happen to you," he said to the poor souls. "All you have to do is breathe in deeply. It strengthens the lungs. Breathing in prevents infectious diseases. It is a good way of disinfecting." They asked what was going to happen to them. He told them: "The men will have to build houses and roads. But women do not have to do that; they can do housework or help in the kitchen." For some of the poor wretches, this did the trick; it was enough to get them into the gas chambers without resistance. Most knew the truth. The stench made it clear what their fate was. They walked into the gas chambers along a narrow staircase, most saying nothing, forced forward by those behind them. A Jewish woman of around forty, with eyes like coals, cursed her murderers. Encouraged by the lashes from Captain Wirth's whip, she too disappeared into the gas chamber. Many prayed, whilst others asked: "Who will give us water to wash the dead?"'[10]

Kurt Gerstein, SS-Officer, 1942

His reports and those of others would not bring help for the victims. Sometimes the horrific stories were not believed. Misunderstanding, disbelief and a lack of will prevented any help from being provided to the persecuted Jews. Intervention was not part of the allied strategy, who put overall victory above everything.

7. The end of the war, the end of persecution

As the defeat of the Third Reich became apparent and the Red Army approached, the Nazis realised that the mass graves should not be discovered. Orders were given to erase all traces of the Nazi crimes. Bodies were dug up and incinerated. Remains of extermination camps were razed to the ground. It did not prove possible to eradicate all evidence of mass murder. Auschwitz was liberated by the Red Army on 27 January 1945. It became the symbol for the Holocaust.

In the final phase of the war, the German SS and police committed countless atrocities. They murdered prisoners. They forced the survivors in concentration camps to head west. Sometimes by train, but often by foot, in terrible conditions. Even in retreat, the SS guards did not hesitate to murder the weak or those who tried to flee. Many people also died from sickness and disease. These journeys have since become known as the Death Marches.

The survivors ended up in camps in the West, where they were eventually liberated by the Allies. Many still died from illness and exhaustion after that. Others had to live with the memory of the suffering they had been through and the realisation that many of their family members and friends had not survived the persecution.

Living Jewish culture in Europe had been wiped out, but anti-Semitism persisted in post-war society. The survivors needed a great deal of courage to build a new life in Europe, Israel or elsewhere. For many, it was too harrowing to tell of their experiences. In recent decades, attempts have been made to record their testimonies and memories as much as possible.

8. Aftermath and justice

The number of perpetrators of this genocide, those who organised it and the perpetrators of the actual crimes themselves, runs into hundreds of thousands. From 22 November 1945 until 31 August 1946, the Nuremberg trials took place in Germany, lasting nine months. The trials were held on a grand scale, with four judges and four prosecuting counsels, from the United States, Great Britain, the Soviet Union and France. The court sat 403 times, heard testimonies from 166 witnesses and studied thousands of statements and hundreds of thousands of documents. 24 men were tried, as they were considered to be the most important war criminals. 12 of them were sentenced to death. At that time, the terms genocide and Holocaust were not yet in use. The suspects were accused of war crimes and crimes against humanity. Since 1946, there have been numerous trials, but even in 2011, many suspects remain unpunished.

Internationally, the trial against Adolf Eichmann in Jerusalem in 1961 was particularly significant. Eichmann had escaped to South America after the war, ending up in Argentina, where he was kidnapped by the Israeli secret service. He was sentenced to death. His trial brought the Holocaust to international attention. The important question of individual responsibility for shared guilt and crimes was raised loud and clear for all who wished to hear it.

Specific character

In total, approximately 5.7 million Jews were murdered. The Nazi goal to murder all Jews was not achieved. Despite the unfathomable numbers, this is an important fact in determining the meaning of the Holocaust. It is this goal of murdering all Jews that, together with the murderous anti-Semitism, the mass executions, the rationally orchestrated operations, deportation trains, and industrially organised extermination camps, defines the specific character of the Holocaust.

Nuremberg trials. Front row: Goering, Hess, Von Ribbentrop, Keitel, Rosenberg, Frank, Frick, Streicher, Funk, Schacht.
Back row: Donitz, Raeder, Von Schirach, Sauckel, Jodl, Von Papen, Seyss-Inquart, Speer, Von Neurath and Fritsche
Source: National Archives and Records Administration

THIRD REICH 1942

SWEDEN

BALTIC STATES
● Riga

DENMARK

LITHUANIA

Vilnius
Ponary ★●

POLAND
Chelmno
★
Treblinka
★

BELARUS

Westerbork
★
●Amsterdam

Berlin
●

WARTHELAND
Lódz
●

Warsaw
●

Belzec
★★
Sobibor

NETHERLANDS

Majdanek
Lublin ● ★

Buchenwald
★
Theresienstadt
★

GENERAL GOVERNMENT

Kiev
★●
Babi Jar

BELGIUM

Auschwitz
Kraków
●

Lviv
●

Prague
●

UKRAINE

FRANCE

Nuremberg
●

BOHEMIA AND MORAVIA

SLOVAKIA

★ extermination camp / Holocaust location
border of the Third Reich 1942
border of the eastern occupied territories
neutral countries

Dachau
★

Vienna
★

AUSTRIA

HUNGARY
Budapest
●

ROMANIA

Geographical maps in this book include names that are mostly mentioned in the text.

Adolf Eichmann (1906-1962)
The SS officer and *Regierungsrat* Adolph Eichmann, head of the RSHA subdepartment IV B 4, was responsible for the organisation of the deportation of the Jews outside of the Reich and the Soviet Union. After the war, Eichmann succeeded in escaping to South America. At the start of the 1960s, he was captured and sentenced to death. His trial would again bring the Holocaust to international attention.

Joseph Goebbels (1897-1945)
Goebbels was Minister of Propaganda and one of the most powerful men in Nazi Germany. After Hitler's suicide, Goebbels refused to rule the Third Reich and also committed suicide, with his wife and children.

Reinhard Heydrich (1904-1942)
Heydrich, head of the Security Police and Security Service, was tasked with leading the execution of the *Endlösung*. He informed leading officials from ministries and administrative bodies in the east of the need to cooperate in the murder of all European Jews. On 27 March 1942, Heydrich fell victim to an attack by the Czech resistance.

Heinrich Himmler (1900-1945)
Himmler, *Reichsführer* of the SS, took over overall supervision of the *Endlösung*. Before he could be brought to justice, he committed suicide.

Adolf Hitler (1889-1945)
Hitler, born in Austria, was the leader of the National Socialist Party. As Chancellor and head of state of Nazi Germany, he is considered to be responsible for the death of millions of people, including 5.7 million Jews and an estimated 500,000 Roma and Sinti. Hitler committed suicide in Berlin.

Adolf Hitler
Source: Beeldbank WO2 — NIOD

Glossary

Aktion Reinhardt	Code name for the systematic annihilation of all European Jews. Once caught, Jews were murdered on the spot or deported to three specially designed extermination camps.
Anti-Semitism	Deep-rooted hatred of the Jews that developed since the start of Christianity. Accusations repeatedly resurfaced that the Jews were responsible for Christ's death.
Concentration camps	Camps where people were forced to live in poor conditions as a means of isolating specific groups from society.
Deportation	Forced transport, in horrendous conditions, often to extermination camps in Poland.
Endlösung	According to the Nazi regime, Jews were an inferior race, and considered to be a 'problem'. The eradication of Jews from society was seen as the final solution to this problem.
Extermination camps	Intended exclusively for the large-scale killing of people, part of *Aktion Reinhardt*.
General Government	Part of Poland, including cities such as Warsaw, Lviv and Kraków, governed as a protectorate. The General Government was occupied but not annexed to Nazi Germany.
Ghettos	The forced concentration of Jews in sealed off overpopulated city districts, with few amenities. While waiting for deportation, Jews were forced to work.
Jewish Council	Representatives of the Jewish population designated by the Germans to take care of internal governance, but otherwise completely dependent on the Germans.

Kristallnacht	Pogrom in which storm troopers from the *Sturmabteilung* and other party members vandalised and robbed Jewish shops and attacked and even murdered Jews on the night of 9 to 10 November 1938.
Nuremberg Laws	Race laws, announced by the National Socialist German Workers Party (NSDAP) on 15 September 1935, according to which the 'Jewish race' was subordinated to the 'Aryan' race.
Partisans	Resistance movement; in the Soviet Union, partisans were executed by *Einsatzgruppen*.
Pogrom	Organised attacks of violence against minority groups, in this case against the Jews.
SS	*Schutzstaffel*, part of the NSDAP, considered to be an elite unit.
Third Reich	Nazi Germany, also known as the Thousand Year Empire, during Adolf Hitler's regime.

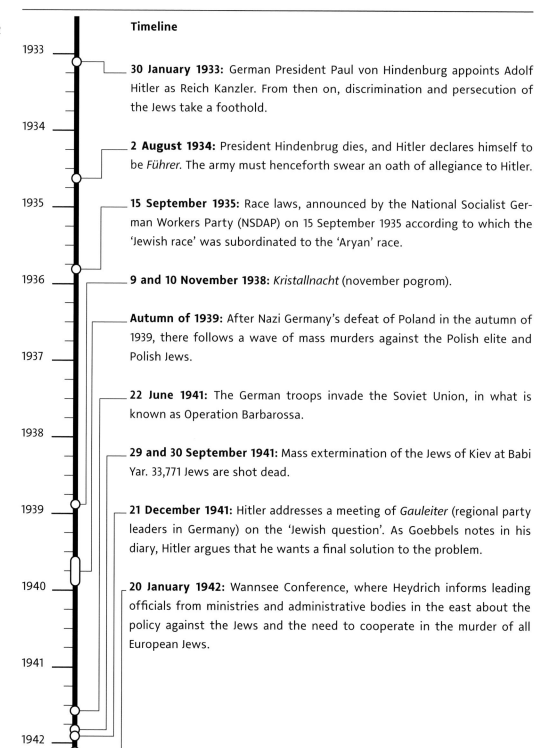

Timeline

1933

30 January 1933: German President Paul von Hindenburg appoints Adolf Hitler as Reich Kanzler. From then on, discrimination and persecution of the Jews take a foothold.

1934

2 August 1934: President Hindenbrug dies, and Hitler declares himself to be *Führer*. The army must henceforth swear an oath of allegiance to Hitler.

1935

15 September 1935: Race laws, announced by the National Socialist German Workers Party (NSDAP) on 15 September 1935 according to which the 'Jewish race' was subordinated to the 'Aryan' race.

1936

9 and 10 November 1938: *Kristallnacht* (november pogrom).

Autumn of 1939: After Nazi Germany's defeat of Poland in the autumn of 1939, there follows a wave of mass murders against the Polish elite and Polish Jews.

1937

22 June 1941: The German troops invade the Soviet Union, in what is known as Operation Barbarossa.

1938

29 and 30 September 1941: Mass extermination of the Jews of Kiev at Babi Yar. 33,771 Jews are shot dead.

1939

21 December 1941: Hitler addresses a meeting of *Gauleiter* (regional party leaders in Germany) on the 'Jewish question'. As Goebbels notes in his diary, Hitler argues that he wants a final solution to the problem.

1940

20 January 1942: Wannsee Conference, where Heydrich informs leading officials from ministries and administrative bodies in the east about the policy against the Jews and the need to cooperate in the murder of all European Jews.

1941

1942

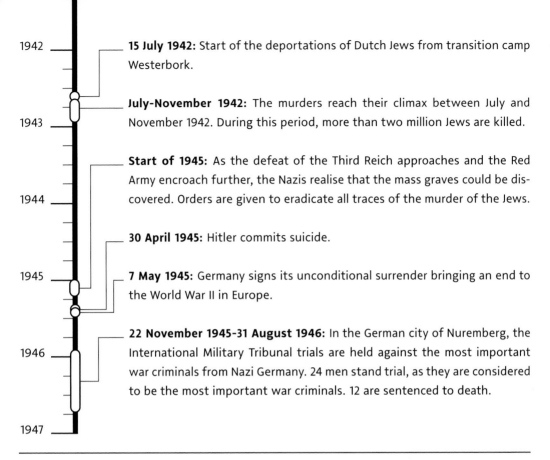

15 July 1942: Start of the deportations of Dutch Jews from transition camp Westerbork.

July-November 1942: The murders reach their climax between July and November 1942. During this period, more than two million Jews are killed.

Start of 1945: As the defeat of the Third Reich approaches and the Red Army encroach further, the Nazis realise that the mass graves could be discovered. Orders are given to eradicate all traces of the murder of the Jews.

30 April 1945: Hitler commits suicide.

7 May 1945: Germany signs its unconditional surrender bringing an end to the World War II in Europe.

22 November 1945-31 August 1946: In the German city of Nuremberg, the International Military Tribunal trials are held against the most important war criminals from Nazi Germany. 24 men stand trial, as they are considered to be the most important war criminals. 12 are sentenced to death.

1942
1943
1944
1945
1946
1947

Notes

1 Schelvis, J. (2007). *Binnen de Poorten. Een verslag van twee jaar Duitse vernietigings- en concentratiekampen.* Amsterdam. pp. 25-30.

2 Kershaw, I. (2000). *Hitler 1936-1945, Nemesis.* New York. p. 339.

3 Melching, W. and M. Stuivenga (eds.) (2011). *Joseph Goebbels, Hitlers Spindoctor. Een selectie uit de dagboeken 1933-1945.* Amsterdam.

4 Schelvis, J. (2010). *Ooggetuigen van Sobibor.* Amsterdam. pp. 125-126.

5 Dwork, D. and R.J. van Pelt (2002). *Holocaust. A History.* New York. p. 279.

6 Schelvis, J. (2010). *Ooggetuigen.* pp. 60-61.

7 As cited in Pohl, D. (2003). *Verfolgung und Massenmord in der NS-Zeit 1933-1945.* Darmstadt. p.95.

8 With thanks to the Anne Frank House and Herinneringscentrum Kamp Westerbork, www.kampwesterbork.nl/nl/jodenvervolging/het-oosten/auschwitz/

9 Levi, P. (1947) *Is this a man.* London.

10 Friedländer, S. and K. Gerstein (1969). *The Ambiguity of Good.* New York. pp. 109-110.

Family of deportees on the road
Source: Armin T. Wegner Collectie, Armenian National Institute

The Armenian Genocide, 1915

Uğur Ümit Üngör

'*Either the Armenians would eliminate the Turks or the Turks would eliminate the Armenians. I didn't hesitate for one moment when confronted with this dilemma. My Turkish identity won out over my profession. I thought: we must destroy them before they destroy us. If you ask me how I as a doctor could commit murder, my answer is simple: the Armenians had become dangerous microbes in the body of this country. And surely it is a doctor's duty to kill bacteria?*'[1]
Dr Mehmed Reshid (1873-1919), Governor of Diyarbekir during the genocide

'*The Turkish government began deporting the Armenian community in Sivas in convoys. Each neighbourhood was given a certain date for leaving. On the first day I watched in amazement at the crowds waiting to be deported, an endless throng of people stretching from one end of the street to the other. The pushing and shoving of the mules and the creaking of the carts made an ear-deafening noise. Men wearing hats to protect them from the sun walked alongside the carts, followed by women wearing white head scarves. Each had a task: one person was holding the cart, another the reins of the mule and yet another was watching over the family possessions. The children walked on either side of their parents as if they were setting off on a pleasant journey. At each end of the caravan rode mounted Turkish policemen, leading and controlling the convoy. The Turkish neighbours watched the spectacle from their windows. The streets were packed with Turkish children who ran alongside the caravan calling us names, giving the occasional prod to a mule or throwing stones at us.*'[2]
Shahen Derderian (1907-1984), Sivas genocide survivor

Introduction

In the early 20th century, the Ottoman Empire stretched across three continents. It was largely an agricultural society, the Sultan's reign was far from absolute and in some remote regions local rulers enjoyed a comparatively large degree of autonomy. At the height of its power the empire counted 29 provinces, each subdivided into towns and cities, districts and villages. Ottoman society included a huge diversity of ethnic and religious groups, who based their identity largely on their religious convictions: people were viewed first and foremost as Muslim, Jew or Christian.

The Ottoman Armenians formed a mixed community: a rich Armenian trader in Istanbul may have spoken several languages and travelled abroad frequently, whereas a poor Armenian peasant from one of the villages in Eastern Anatolia may only have spoken Armenian and barely travelled at all. Most Armenians were Apostolic Christians, although in some cities they were Protestant or Catholic. Armenians lived mainly in the eastern provinces, in a huge area stretching from Sivas in the west to Van in the east, and from Trabzon in the north to Aleppo in the south. In this territory they lived side by side with Kurds, Turks, Arabs and others.

Just before the First World War there were around two million Christian Armenians living in the Ottoman Empire. In the spring of 1915, the Ottoman government initiated measures which signalled the start of the persecution of the Armenians in the Ottoman Empire. By the end of the First World War only a fraction of the pre-war Armenian community was left in the region and today there are hardly any Armenians living in the Anatolian interior. These bare facts sum up the complex history of the Armenian genocide in a nutshell.

1. Historical background

The Ottoman Empire reached the height of its power in the 16th and 17th centuries, when it grew from a small princedom to become the single most important state in the Mediterranean and the Near East. However, external pressure from Western imperialism combined with internal turmoil caused by separatist movements put an end to the empire's growth. Technological innovation and economic development allowed Western Europe to surpass the Ottoman Empire both economically and in terms of military power. The most significant Western concept to find its way into the Ottoman Empire was undoubtedly that of nationalism. The number of nationalist parties in the empire grew rapidly and nationalism went on to become the most serious problem in Ottoman domestic politics.

The decline of the Ottoman Empire

The Ottoman Empire began to lose territory rapidly. In 1821 Greece unilaterally declared independence from the Empire, followed in 1875 by Serbia, Montenegro, Bosnia, and Moldavia. After the Russo-Turkish War of 1877-1878, the Ottoman Empire was forced to grant independence to Serbia, Romania and Montenegro as well as some degree of autonomy to Bulgaria. In 1882, Great Britain occupied first Cyprus and then Egypt. The remainder of

Ottoman North Africa was lost between 1830 and 1912, as France occupied Algeria in 1830 and Tunisia in 1881, and Italy invaded Libya in 1912.[3]

The Ottoman Armenians made considerable economic progress throughout the 19th century. The Armenian financial and industrial elite and the urban middle classes and skilled craftsmen were treated relatively mildly by the Ottoman government. The economic elite financed social organisations such as schools, hospitals and charities. Armenians became imperial architects, armourers, watchmakers and cabinet makers; they were responsible for the Imperial Mint, the cannon and shipbuilding industries, and they dominated trade. Armenian businesses based in Istanbul successfully branched out to European cities such as Marseille and Manchester. As a result of this renaissance the Armenian elite gained economic power, although no political power.

Armenian economic superiority

Of the 166 Ottoman importers, 141 were Armenian and 13 Turkish.

Of the 9,800 shopkeepers and craftsmen, 6,800 were Armenian and 2,550 were Turkish.

Of the 150 exporters, 127 were Armenian and 23 Turkish.

Of the 153 industrialists, 130 were Armenian and 20 were Turkish.

Of the 37 bankers throughout the country, no fewer than 32 were Armenian.

Krikor Zohrab, Armenian parliamentarian and writer, 1913

This disparate economic development and modernisation led to envy on the part of the Ottoman Turks. The Turkish political elite in Istanbul in particular took exception to the success of the Armenian merchants.[4]

The decline of the Ottoman Empire led to major political strife. The autocratic Sultan Abdulhamid II (1842-1918) enforced a policy of centralisation, which provoked feelings of radicalism and separatism. This radicalism pervaded every level of society and education. Ottoman intellectuals disseminated European nationalistic theories at military, political and medical educational institutions. In 1889, the resulting generation of well-educated public servants and military cadets established the Committee of Union and Progress (*İttihad ve Terakki Cemiyeti*, CUP). The goal of this illegal committee was to restore the constitution of 1876. Most of these Young Turks (*Jeunes Turcs*) lived in Paris, spreading propaganda against the Sultan. Major CUP members were party leader Mehmed Talaat (1874-1921), Major İsmail Enver (1881-1922), and activist Dr Bahaeddin Shakir (1874-1922).[5]

2. Ideology

The ideology of the CUP represented three main streams: Ottomanism, Islamism and Turkism. This trichotomy was formulated by historian Yusuf Akçura (1876-1935) who, in 1904, wrote the influential manifesto *Three Types of Politics*. In this pamphlet Akçura stated that the Ottoman

Enver Pascha
Türkischer Kriegsminister

Nicola Perscheid, Berlin

Ismail Enver Pasha
Source: Armenian Genocide Museum Institute

political elite was standing on the threshold of rejecting Ottomanism and Islamism: the first through religious discord, the second through the well-developed nationalism among non-Turkish Muslims such as Albanians. Akçura's conclusion was that people should accept Turkish nationalism as their guiding ideological principle. He found these thoughts echoed in the work of Ziyâ Gökalp (1876-1924), a sociologist who wrote a great deal about Turkish nationalism throughout his career. His most important writings cover the Turkification of the Ottoman Empire, for example in the fields of language, religion, public life, ethics and economy. In his articles and poems, Gökalp extolled the virtues of Turkish culture and history in particular and expressed open hostility towards non-Turkish sections of the population.

The decline of the state radicalised both the internal political culture and the ideology of the CUP. One of the most radical factions developed a profoundly ethnic Turkish nationalism driven by a collective hatred of Armenians.[6]

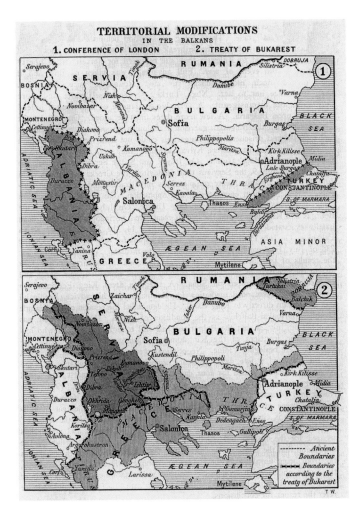

Territorial Modifications in the Balkans
Source: *The Other Balkan Wars: A 1913 Carnegie Endowment Inquiry in Retrospect*, George F. Kennan (Washington, DC; Carnegie Endowment for International Peace, 1993), p. 70

3. Causes of the genocide

The genocide of the Ottoman Armenians was the result of three important factors: the loss of the Balkan War and territory in 1912-1913, the coup by the Young Turks of 23 January 1913, and the start of the First World War.

On 17 October 1912, Serbia, Montenegro, Greece and Bulgaria declared war on the Ottoman Empire. The Ottoman army was unprepared and ill-equipped to fight. Following the Bulgarian offensive in November 1913, the Ottoman army retreated to the trenches 30 kilometres west of Istanbul. The attack was repelled and the capital Istanbul remained under Ottoman control. Further fighting led to the complete and permanent loss of the Balkan Peninsula. The Treaty of London, signed on 30 May 1913, was regarded as a watershed for the Ottoman Empire. It had a deep and traumatic impact on Ottoman society. The loss of major Ottoman cities, personal possessions and human life, and the dismay regarding the inadequacy of the army had wounded the pride of the Ottoman elite. Ottoman society, culture and identity had been dealt a heavy blow.

From 1913 onwards, nationalists felt that the idea of a unified 'Ottoman' identity was no longer realistic. The war had also reinforced the myth of a 'stab in the back' by the Ottoman Christians. Tensions mounted among politicians, with the CUP launching provocations, accusations, curses and threats at Ottoman Bulgarians, Greeks and Armenians in Parliament.

Revanchism

The loss of the Balkan War brought a culture of revanchism. In a letter to his wife on 8 May 1913, Enver wrote: 'If I could only tell you about the atrocities committed by the enemy... at just a stone's throw from Istanbul, then you would understand what is going on in the minds of Muslims far away. Yet our anger is growing: revenge, revenge, revenge, there is no other word for it!'[7]

A second milestone was the coup by the Young Turks of 23 January 1913. The Young Turks, never elected to power, used a violent coup to install a dictator. Parliament was forced into silence, members of the opposition were intimidated or killed, and the Young Turks muscled their way into the Ottoman state bureaucracy. The foundations of their rule lay in a brutal war. The coup led to a concentration of power in which the Young Turks transformed the multi-ethnic Ottoman society into a homogenous Turkish nation state. The new regime was not widely supported by the population and any danger of a counter-revolution was warded off by sheer violence.[8]

The Young Turk regime that ruled from 1913 until 1918 comprised a circle of around 50 men led by the 'duo' Talaat and Enver. Local party barons and Young Turk provincial governors were quite influential on a national level. There was intense rivalry within the Young Turk dictatorship, particularly between Enver as military commander and Talaat as head of the civilian administration. These rivalries would later influence the course of the Armenian genocide.

However, the most important trigger for the genocide was the start of the First World War. On 2 August 1914, one day after Germany had declared war on Russia, Germany and the Ottoman Empire signed an agreement for close collaboration and mobilisation. On 29 October 1914, without an official declaration of war, Enver ordered the Ottoman Navy to shell the Russian coast, upon which the allied states declared war on the Ottoman Empire. From 11 November 1914, the Ottoman Empire was officially at war with Russia, France and Great Britain.

The Young Turks had deliberately engineered an armed confrontation. This war of aggression was part of their strategy to achieve long-lasting security and economic development and eventually national recovery. In other words, the CUP hoped that participation in the war would offer a radical solution to the problems of the Empire.[9]

Nonetheless, the Ottoman Army suffered heavy losses. Driven by ambition and expansionism, Enver launched a number of invasions, with catastrophic results. He attributed these disasters to 'Armenian betrayal'. From January 1915 onwards, the Armenians were used as a scapegoat: Turkish-nationalistic propaganda accused the Armenians of treason, called for a boycott of Armenian businesses and spread horror stories of alleged crimes by Armenian activists. Armenian newspapers were shut down and prominent Armenians arrested. The more hopeless the war became, the more radical the persecution of the Armenians.[10]

4. Nature and course of the genocide

The Armenian genocide was a consistent process of destruction, with mass executions, dispossession, deportation, forced assimilation, state-induced famine and destruction of material culture.

The mass executions of the economic, religious, political and intellectual elite resulted in a 'beheading' of Armenian society. The large-scale razzia in Istanbul on 24 April 1915 became a blueprint for the rounding up of the Armenian elite — middle-aged and elderly men with influence, wealth and status — living in the many cities across the vast empire. They were arrested, imprisoned, tortured and finally murdered. The destruction of the Armenian intelligentsia proceeded at a staggering pace: the entire higher echelon of the community was eliminated in a matter of weeks.[11]

Executed in public square
Source: Armenian National Institute

Mass murder in Diyarbekir

On Sunday 30 May 1915, the entire Armenian elite — 636 dignitarie including the bishop — in the south-eastern city of Diyarbekir was handcuffed and taken to the Tigris by members of the militia. Once they reached the river they were loaded onto large rafts, supposedly for transportation to the south. The militia sailed the notables downstream to a gorge where they moored the rafts. The victims were robbed of their money and taken away in groups of six, then stripped of all clothing and valuables and murdered by men recruited by the governor, using axes, daggers and guns. The bodies were then dumped into the river.

The Armenian genocide represents one of the foremost examples of asset transfer — economic dispossession — in modern history. The Young Turk government passed new laws providing for the annexation of Armenian businesses and trades. On 10 June 1915, the government passed a law establishing the Abandoned Property Commission (*Emval-ı Metruke Komisyonu*) which was tasked with organising the daily carrying out of seizures. This was a full-frontal attack on the Armenian economy, as all Armenian property was now officially transferred to the state. A new

Deportation of the Armenians on the Baghdad railway
Source: Armenian Genocide Museum Institute

law followed on 26 September 1915 which delegated the implementation of the seizures to the Ministries of Internal Affairs, Justice and Finance, who would keep a detailed overview. Law was an instrument of power for the Young Turks, as these two laws gave them access to vast economic resources, including properties, factories, workshops and studios. These measures led to mass poverty among the Armenians.

Robbery

'Leave all your belongings — your furniture, your bedding, your artefacts. Close your shops and businesses with everything inside. Your doors will be sealed with special stamps. On your return, you will get everything you left behind. Do not sell property or any expensive item. Buyers and sellers alike will be liable for legal action. Put your money in a bank in the name of a relative who is out of the country. Make a list of everything you own, including livestock, and give it to the specified official so that all your things can be returned to you later. You have ten days to comply with this ultimatum.'[12]

Government notice displayed in public places in Kayseri, 15 June 1915

On 23 May 1915, Talaat gave the official order for the final deportation of the entire Armenian population. Some Armenians had already been isolated from their settlements by deportation, and this new order led to the deportation of virtually all Armenians to the inhospitable Syrian desert city of Der el-Zor. In an attempt to camouflage the deportations as legal, Talaat drew up the temporary 'Dispatchment and Settlement Law'. This law came into force on 29 May, although deportations had already begun. The daily administration for the deportations was transferred to the Directorate for the Settlement of Tribes and Immigrants (İskân-ı Aşâir ve Muhacirîn Müdüriyeti), under the authority of the army. Talaat was kept informed of progress via telegraph correspondence and the assistance of local officials.[13]

These measures led to the mobilisation of a huge peasant population which lived for the most part in the Anatolian countryside. Some Armenians had a few days to get ready to leave, while others received just a few hours' notice.

Deportation from Erzurum

In early 1915, 40,000 Armenians living in the city of Erzurum were deported to Der el-Zor. The German Consul in Erzurum reported in no uncertain terms that the deportation would end in 'an absolute extermination' (eine absolute Ausrottung). And indeed, many Armenians had already died or were seriously weakened even before the convoy from Erzurum had reached the provincial border. Once they reached the city of Kemah the survivors of the march were slaughtered and their bodies thrown into the Euphrates. The total number of Armenians from Erzurum that actually reached Der el-Zor was probably less than 200, a destruction rate of 99.3 percent.

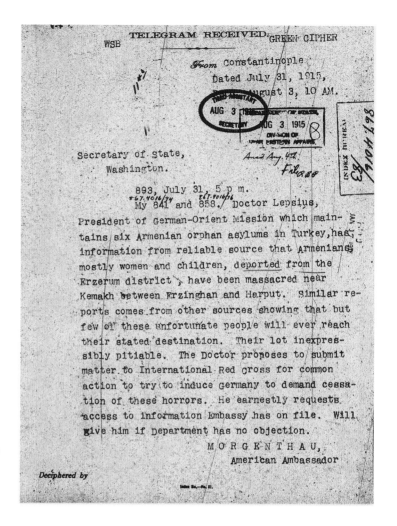

Message from the American ambassador Morgenthau on the deportations from Ezurum, 31 July 1915
Source: Armenian National Institute

By July 1915, the entire Armenian population had been uprooted, bound for the Syrian desert. In some cases people had to travel over 1,000 kilometres through the scorching heat of the merciless Eastern Anatolian summer, which proved a death sentence for many. Moreover, the Young Turk leaders were well aware that the chances of survival in the desert of the Der el-Zor region were virtually nil. For children, the elderly and pregnant women in particular the deportations were nothing less than death marches.[14]

When reaching the Syrian desert, they found nothing had been arranged for them. In early 1916, there was a famine in Der el-Zor, to which the Young Turk authorities remained indifferent. In the summer of 1916 Talaat even decided too many Armenians had survived the journey to Der el-Zor, and he instructed his district governor to herd thousands of Armenians into caves and kill them.

Armenian orphans collected in the desert of Der el-Zor, 1919
Source: Armenian Genocide Museum-Institute

Another important aspect of the destruction of the Ottoman Armenians was the forced loss of identity. Women and children had to renounce their Christian faith and convert to Islam, as part of a large-scale attack on Armenian culture. Numerous women and children were abducted during the deportations and forced to convert. In cities like Konya and Beirut, Armenian children were placed in huge Muslim orphanages where they were given Turkish names and were only allowed to speak Turkish. As a result, many forgot their Armenian identity. The abductions and conversions were aimed at marginalising the Armenians and eradicating their culture and collective identity.[15]

Finally, the material culture of the Armenians was obliterated. The Young Turks damaged and destroyed Armenian churches and removed Armenian inscriptions from buildings. This destruction was aimed at eliminating all traces of Armenian cultural and religious life from the Ottoman

Empire. Many medieval Armenian monasteries, such as Narekavank, Varakavank, Arakelots Vank, Surp Garabed and Surp Khach were demolished by the Young Turk regime. The destruction served a dual purpose: it made it appear that the Armenians had never existed, while ensuring that survivors, if any, had nothing to return to.

All traces wiped out

In 1914 the Armenian community owned 2,600 churches, 450 monasteries, and 2,000 schools. At the end of the war, roughly 3,000 Armenian settlements (villages, towns, neighbourhoods) had been depopulated, their inhabitants wiped out. Today there are hardly any Armenians living in Turkey, except in Istanbul. The present Armenian community has six churches, but not a single school or monastery remains.[16]

---

5. Perpetrators, victims, bystanders

5.1 Perpetrators

The most important perpetrators in the process of the genocide were the Ottoman Turks and Kurds, which included highly educated intellectuals as well as labourers and unemployed illiterates. Talaat, leader of the Young Turk party and Minister of Home Affairs, engineered the genocide, rationalising it by accusing the Armenians collectively of high treason, sabotage and disloyalty. In 1916 he published a four-volume book entitled *The Armenian Aspirations and Revolutionary Movements*.[17] This book contains manipulated photographs of alleged Armenian 'terrorists' in each city of the Ottoman Empire. Every photograph tells the same story: Ottoman policemen and Young Turk paramilitaries gathered behind a group of Armenian men who, with heads bowed, are standing in front of a pile of guns and bombs. And the caption invariably reads: 'Armenian revolutionaries arrested with their weapons'. The lies spread by the Young Turks and supported by the German department for war propaganda were influential and are still disseminated and believed by many people today.

Talaat's true motives were ideological and pragmatic, and he had both material and immaterial interests. In a confidential conversation with the German Consul he admitted that 'the Ottoman government intends to use the Great War to effectively do away with its internal enemies, the indigenous Christians of every denomination, without being disturbed by foreign diplomatic intervention'. In internal secret correspondence Talaat left it in no doubt that the purpose of the genocide was to 'Turkify' Anatolia by driving out all Armenians.

Talaat was quite clear to the American Ambassador Henry Morgenthau about his intentions:

'I have asked you to come today so that I can explain our position on the whole of the Armenian subject. We base our objections to the Armenians on three distinct grounds.

In the first place they have enriched themselves at the expense of Turks. In the second place they are determined to domineer over us and to establish a separate state. In the third place they have openly encouraged our enemies. They have assisted the Russians in the Caucasus and our failure there is largely explained by their actions. We have therefore come to the irrevocable decision that we shall make them powerless before this war is ended... It is no use for you to argue, we have already disposed of three quarters of the Armenians; there are none at all left in Bitlis, Van and Erzurum. The hatred between the Turks and the Armenians is now so intense that we have got to finish with them. If we don't, they will plan their revenge... We care nothing about the commercial loss. We have figured all that out and know that it will not exceed five million Turkish Lira. We don't worry about that. I have asked you to come here so as to let you know that our Armenian policy is absolutely fixed and that nothing can change it. We will not have the Armenians anywhere in Anatolia... No Armenian can be our friend after what we have done to them.'[18]

5.2 Victims

Throughout their history the Armenians suffered periods of persecution, and many Armenians saw the genocide as yet another 'regular' Ottoman pogrom. The victims of the genocide came from various classes, areas and backgrounds and had a wide political and ethnic diversity. Internal unity was never a characteristic of the Armenian community. For this reason the genocide remained incomprehensible to many: many intellectuals who were arrested on 24 April 1915 wondered what they had in common with their fellow detainees. One of the few Armenians who did foresee the catastrophe was the journalist Aram Andonian (1875-1952). In 1913 he wrote that the ethnic nationalism as practised in the Balkans would bring nothing but misery.[19]

The description and definition of the target group of the genocide was continually being changed and adapted. Initially, Talaat ordered the deportation of the Apostolic Armenians. As the summer of 1915 progressed there was some confusion as to the definition of an Armenian. This led to the inclusion of Protestant and Catholic Armenians in the group to be persecuted, followed later even by Armenians who had converted to Islam. The Armenian identity was radicalised. The destruction became targeted at the abstract identity of the group: eventually every Armenian, whether loyal or disloyal, political or apolitical, was a target and a potential victim. This is what makes the destruction of the Armenians genocide.

5.3 Bystanders

The most important bystanders in the country itself were Turks and Kurds, who were involved both as collaborators and rebels. There was little ideological background to the Kurdish participation — the Armenians had even helped the Kurds in their struggle against Turkish nationalism. Opportunism, incitement and coercion lay at the foundation of their participation in the genocide. Kurds received payment for providing information to the Young Turk elite about Armenians who had gone into hiding. However, the Kurd sheikhs explicitly condemned the bloodshed. Government-appointed imams also encouraged Muslims to murder Armenians. The propaganda extended to pseudo-Islamic rhetoric stating that a heavenly reward awaited all who killed Armenians. Many uneducated peasants and naive believers were swayed by this religiously inspired hate speech.[20]

There were also foreign eyewitnesses to the genocide. The initial response of the international community was one of shock and incredulity and there were vehement protests against the events. The wave of persecutions in the spring of 1915 prompted the allies to make a joint declaration condemning the massacres. The declaration criticised the 'crimes of Turkey against humanity and civilization' and promised 'that they will hold personally responsible [...] all members of the Ottoman government and those of their agents who are implicated in such massacres'.[21]

During the war England published the *Blue Book*, a collection of eyewitness accounts of the treatment of Armenians. The book was anonymised to protect the people involved, and for this reason it was condemned as anti-Turkish propaganda. Later, the original version with a long list of names and no blanks was discovered in the British archives. In 2005, an unabridged edition of the collection was published.[22]

Germans and Austrians could move about freely and had privileged access to military zones where normal citizens were not allowed. Consequently, their confidential internal consular reports on the Ottomans may well provide the most truthful account of daily events. The German response to the Armenian genocide was ambivalent. Within German politics there was tension between the elite, whose task it was to serve the larger military interests, and lower-ranking soldiers and officials who were directly confronted with the atrocities. German soldiers and consuls regularly spoke of *Ausrottung, Vernichtungspolitik*, and *Rassenmord* (eradication, policy of destruction and race murder). The Austrian officer Pomiankowski called the genocide '*die Ausrottung einer ganzen Nation*' (the eradication of an entire nation). The Austro-Hungarian ambassador Johann von Pallavicini (1848-1941) called the genocide '*eine gänzliche Ausrottung*' (a total eradication) and a '*Politik der Exterminierung*' (policy of extermination).

In the autumn of 1915 a group of around 50 Germans responded to the genocide by signing a joint petition putting pressure on the German government. The petition argued that the genocide had caused serious damage and urged the German government to stop and prevent deportations. The petition made mention of economic arguments, humanitarian principles and the reputation of Germany. However, German military and political leaders considered the alliance with Turkey too important and merely voiced a few half-hearted internal protests against Talaat and Enver.[23]

The United States maintained a neutral position until 1917, and their consuls in the major cities

№ 44. ЕЖЕНЕДѢЛЬНЫЙ ЖУРНАЛЪ Цѣна 20 k.

АРМЯНСКІЙ ВѢСТНИКЪ

27 Ноября. ГОДЪ ИЗДАНІЯ Iый 1916 г.

ЖЕРТВЫ ТУРЕЦКИХЪ ЗВѢРСТВЪ.

Трупы армянъ.

МОСКВА.

Weekly Journal, Moscow, 27 November 1916. 'Victims of Turkish cruelties'

witnessed the deportation from the beginning to the end. The American Consul in Harput, for example, wrote a weighty and damning report following field work in the region, and Ambassador Henry Morgenthau wrote about the genocide in his diaries and memoires. On 16 July 1915, Morgenthau reported to Washington that 'harrowing reports of eyewitnesses suggest that *a campaign of race extermination* is in progress under a pretext of reprisal against rebellion'.

American interests in the Ottoman Empire ran from diplomacy and commerce to charity, Christian missions and education. The genocide effectively destroyed their infrastructure: Armenian business and institutions were confiscated, consulates lost skilled personnel, businesses lost investors and board members, banks lost customers and staff and educational institutions lost their teachers. The Americans withdrew from the Ottoman Empire in 1917 and it would be many years before they would once again enter into diplomatic relations with Turkey.[24]

Essentially, it was in the interest of the major powers to continue their business relations

Armenian looking at the human remains at Der el-Zor, 1916
Source: Armenian Genocide Museum-Institute

with the Armenians. However, the impact of the genocide was overwhelming. The Germans were the first to realise this and decided that at the very least, their own interests must not be compromised. After the war, the Americans, French and British forgot their Armenian business partners, rushing to the new Turkey to safeguard their economic interests. On the whole, the efforts of these states were driven by self-interest: they demanded compensation for their financial losses resulting from the genocide and regarded the wholesale destruction of the Armenians as 'regretful'.

6. The survivors

Some Armenians managed to escape the mass destruction. Besides good luck, there were a number of factors that determined their chance of success in surviving the genocide: bribery, conversion, going into hiding, or fleeing.

To start with, bribing the perpetrators was one way of delaying deportation or escaping abuse or murder. Vahram Dadrian (1900-1948) was a boy of 14 when he was deported from the Ankara region. In his diary he describes how time and time again his family managed to survive by using bribes on the long journey. By the time they arrived in Syria they had virtually nothing left, and the once-prosperous Dadrian family was now quite destitute.[25]

In the spring of 1915 it was still possible to escape deportation by converting to Islam. Henry Vartanian, an Armenian from Sivas whose father had been murdered, recounted how a Turkish acquaintance offered shelter to his family during the war, on the condition that they renounce Christianity and spoke the Muslim oath 'There is no God but Allah and Muhammad is his prophet'. The ceremony was carried out, during which the Young Harry was ritually circumcised. He continued his life as Abdurrahmanoğlu Esad.[26]

Many Armenians attempted to go into hiding and wait for the persecutions to pass. Going into hiding involved many risks. The Armenians who thus survived often had to face extreme hardship. Many were tracked down or betrayed and murdered anyway. It was also risky for those offering shelter. The government had sent out a nationwide decree that 'any Muslim harbouring an Armenian would be executed in front of his house and his house burnt down (*bir Ermeniyi tesahüp edecek bir Müslümanın hanesi önünde idam ve hanesi ihrak)*'.[27]

The beginning of the First World War saw a steady flow of refugees on the move, including some 130,000 Armenians who fled to Russia and Persia (now Iran). Among those was the expressionist painter Arshile Gorky (1904-1948), who survived by escaping the country with his mother, first to Russia and then to the United States. After March 1915, escape was no longer possible.

Yet the single most important factor in most survivors' stories was pure chance or luck. Some leading Armenian intellectuals such as Aram Andonian and Michael Shamtanjian (1874-1926) survived the mass executions by a set of coincidences beyond their control. The editor of the liberal newspaper *Zhamanag*, Yervant Odian (1869-1926), for example, escaped the genocide because a Turkish officer in Der el-Zor did not understand his deportation document and sent him back to Anatolia.[28]

7. Aftermath of the genocide

On 31 October 1918, the string of defeats suffered by the Ottoman Empire resulted in an unconditional surrender. That same night the leaders of the CUP escaped to Odessa in a German submarine, fearing they would be captured and brought to justice. This group comprised Enver, Talaat, Cemal, the doctors Bahaeddin Shakir and Nâzım, and two others. The ensuing power vacuum was filled by the new sultan Mehmet V and the liberals. This new government put an immediate stop to anti-Armenian measures. Deported Armenians could now return to their homes and were compensated for their losses.

During this period the genocide received extensive press coverage and was discussed in parliament. Two estimates from the time put the number of deaths at 800,000 and 1.5 million: by the end of 1918 the liberals acknowledged that 800,000 Armenians had been murdered, while according to Armenian organisations the genocide had claimed 1 to 1,5 million victims. On the basis of later studies it can be stated that the number of deaths in the Armenian genocide of 1915 totalled around 1.2 million.

In 1919, the liberal government established a military tribunal charged with investigating war crimes. Research results from this court martial contain crucial information, including confessions, testimonies and telegrams, which has proved invaluable for historical research. The first series of sessions commenced on 5 February 1919 and the tribunal's final sitting took place on 9 February 1920. Soldiers, eyewitnesses, politicians and Muslim clerics were questioned and 42 official and authenticated documents (telegrams, memoranda, declarations, letters and cross-examinations) were unearthed and presented as evidence. The main charge was 'deportation and murder' (*tehcir ve taktil*) implicating the entire cabinet including the ministers, the army and the CUP as a political party. The court's final verdict, handed down on 5 July 1919, was that the Young Turk government had engaged in a systematic attempt to bring about the total destruction of the Armenian people. The entire leadership of the CUP was sentenced to death *in absentia*. However, the perpetrators escaped justice because they had fled abroad and because the Young Turks returned to power under Mustafa Kemal Atatürk in 1923, driving out the surviving Armenians.[29]

Even though the genocide took place almost 100 years ago and all the persons involved have since died, the Armenian genocide continues to play an important role in present-day international politics. The Armenian genocide has left a lasting legacy. From the 1960s the Armenian diaspora worldwide has called for recognition and a public discussion of the genocide. The response of succeeding Turkish governments has been one of denial and trivialisation. This politics of denial can be largely traced back to the pamphlet published by Talaat in 1916. According to supporters of this theory, 'only' 300,000 Armenians were killed; the Armenians were guilty of collective high treason against the state; the deportation was a preventative measure of the state to evacuate Armenians from war zones and there was never any question of systematic and deliberate killing, let alone anti-Armenian persecution.

The surviving family members of the victims felt deeply insulted by these politics of denial, which prompted a violent response from Armenian nationalists in the 1970s. Two terrorist organisations shot and killed dozens of Turkish diplomats, leading to a denial by the Turks in even stronger terms.

After the fall of the Soviet Union, the Armenian Republic had no diplomatic contact with Turkey. American and Swiss attempts at reconciliation stranded on mutual mistrust and hatred. The Turkish-Armenian border remains firmly closed, which has a highly negative impact on the local economy. Moreover, Turkey's entry into the European Union depends in part on the reopening of this border, which in turn also depends on the acknowledgement of the genocide. Time does not always heal: the Armenian genocide is still a key problem in Armenian-Turkish relations.

Genocide Memorial, Yerevan
Source: Wikimedia

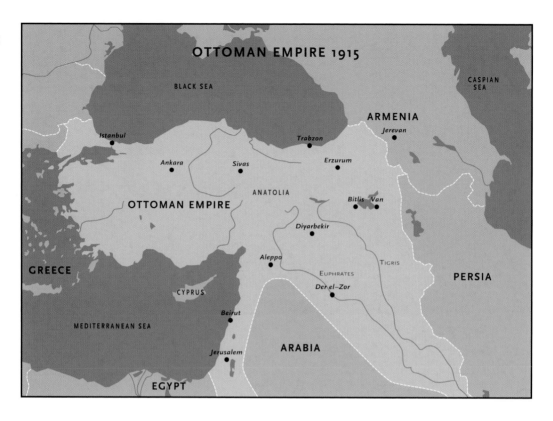

OTTOMAN EMPIRE 1915

BLACK SEA

CASPIAN
SEA

ARMENIA

Istanbul

Trabzon

Jerevan

Ankara

Sivas

Erzurum

ANATOLIA

OTTOMAN EMPIRE

Bitlis *Van*

Diyarbekir

GREECE

Aleppo

TIGRIS

PERSIA

CYPRUS

EUPHRATES

Der el–Zor

Beirut

MEDITERRANEAN SEA

ARABIA

Jerusalem

EGYPT

Sultan Abdulhamid II (1842-1918)
Abdulhamid implemented a desperate policy of centralisation which fuelled radicalism and separatism. This radicalism penetrated deep into society and education.

Mustafa Kemal Atatürk (1881-1938)
Atatürk was a member of the Committee of Union and Progress (CUP) since 1908. After the Turkish War of Independence (against the Allied forces and the Sultan), Atatürk became the first president of the secular Republic of Turkey. He was known for his nationalist politics and many state reforms.

Ismail Enver Pasha (1881-1922)
In 1914 Enver was made Minister of War. In this same year he purged the Ottoman Officer Corps and held secret negotiations with Germany for a military alliance. His political fantasy to unite the Turkish peoples in a pan-Turkish state came to an end when he was killed in an anti-Russian uprising on 4 August 1922.

Şükrü Kaya (1883-1959)
Kaya was one of the persons who bore major responsibility for the mass murder of the Armenians. As head of the administrative apparatus he was responsible for the deportation process, the DSTI, while supervising the construction of concentration camps on the River Euphrates. For many years Kaya held key positions in the Turkish republic under Atatürk.

Dr Bahaeddin Shakir (1877-1922)
Shakir was one of the most influential members of the Central Committee of the CUP. He played a crucial role in the genocide. His proximity to Talaat enabled him to rise quickly through the ranks, which is evidenced by the fact that he was charged with setting up the Special Organisation in 1914. Shakir was killed in Berlin on 17 April 1922.

Mehmed Talaat Pasha (1874-1921)
As Minister of Home Affairs he was responsible for the deportation and destruction of the Armenian people. He resigned his
post on 14 October 1918, two weeks before the surrender. On
15 March 1921, following his escape with other important Young
Turks, he was murdered in Berlin.

Krikor Zohrab (1861-1915)
Zohrab emerged as a gifted and influential writer, politician,
lawyer and philanthropist and was among the best-known Armenians in Istanbul and the world. Heavy political pressure forced
him to flee the country, and he did not return until after the
1908 revolution. He was murdered under orders from Dr Mehmed
Reshid in June 1915.

CUP	Committee for Unity and Progress (*İttihad ve Terakki Cemiyeti*).
APC	Abandoned Property Commission (*Emval-ı Metruke Komisyonu*).
DSTI	Directorate for the Settlement of Tribes and Immigrants *(İskân-ı Aşâir ve Muhacirîn Müdüriyeti)*.
Young Turks (*Jeunes Turcs*)	Members of the CUP, Ottoman intellectuals with European nationalistic theories.
Ottoman Armenians	A varied ethnic group within the Ottoman Empire, lived mainly in the eastern provinces.
Ottoman Empire	Empire established in Western Anatolia around 1300.
Revanchism	A policy of seeking retaliation or revenge.
SO	Special Organisation (*Teşkilât-ı Mahsusa*).

Timeline

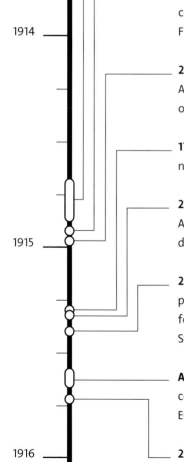

1913

1914

1915

1916

23 January 1913: The Committee for Unity and Progress (CUP) storms the Ottoman Parliament building, seizes power in a bloody coup and installs a dictator.

September-October 1914: The CUP steps up the persecution of the Armenian community through arbitrary war requisitions, arrests, closing schools, banning political parties, and political killings.

11 November 1914: Enver orders the bombing of the Russian coast. The Ottoman Empire is now officially at war with Russia, France and Great Britain.

26 December 1914: Talaat officially orders the resignation of all Armenian government officials and the arrest and deportation of anyone defying these measures.

17 April 1915: Beginning of the siege of Van, an important turning point in Armenian-Turkish relations.

24 April 1915: Starting in the capital Istanbul, thousands of Armenian dignitaries throughout the country are arrested and detained. Most are tortured and eventually killed.

29 May 1915: Talaat passes provisional Law of Deportation (Dispatchment and Settlement Law). This provided legislative cover for the official start of the deportation of Armenians to the Syrian desert.

August 1915: Tens of thousands of deported Armenians are concentrated in a series of camps along the banks of the River Euphrates in the Syrian desert, around Aleppo and in Der el-Zor.

26 September 1915: The 'Law on Abandoned Properties' is ratified by the Ottoman Senate. Armenian property is liquidated and shared out among the Turks.

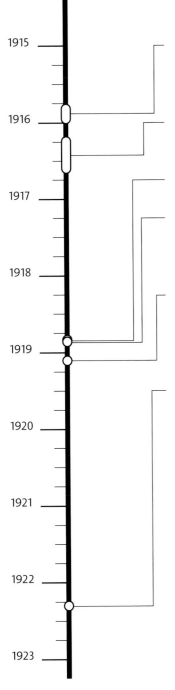

October-December 1915: International help is organised for Armenian deportees.

March-August 1916: Launch of second phase of the Armenian genocide: the mass murder of Armenian deportees in the Syrian desert, in and around Der el-Zor.

31 October 1918: Surrender of the demoralised Ottoman Army.

2 November 1918: The hard core of the CUP burns suitcases full of documents, dissolves the CUP as a political party and escapes in a German submarine to Odessa.

5 February 1919: Establishment of the tribunal in Istanbul that accused the Young Turk party of 'deportation and massacre'. The CUP cabinet is sentenced to death, but negligence and prevarication leads to dismissal of the tribunal.

17 April 1922: Shakir shot dead in Berlin.

Notes

1 Güngör, Salâhattin 'Bir Canlı Tarih Konuşuyor'. In: *Resimli Tarih Mecmuası*, Vol. 4, No. 43 (July 1953), pp. 2444-5.

2 Derderian, Shahen (2008). *Death March: An Armenian Survivor's Memoir of the Genocide of 1915*. Studio City, CA, p. 13.

3 Hanioğlu, M. Şükrü (2008). *A Brief History of the Late Ottoman Empire*. Princeton, NJ.

4 Panossian, Razmik (2006). *The Armenians: From Kings and Priests to Merchants and Commissars*. London, pp. 128-87.

5 Hanioğlu, M. Şükrü (2001). *Preparation for a Revolution: the Young Turks, 1902-1908*. Oxford.

6 Kushner, David (1977). *The Rise of Turkish Nationalism, 1876-1908*. London.

7 Hall, Richard C. (2000). *The Balkan Wars, 1912-1913: Prelude to the First World War*. London.

8 Gawrych, George W. 'The Culture and Politics of Violence in Turkish society, 1903-14'. In: *Middle Eastern Studies*, Vol. 22, No. 3 (1986), pp. 307-30.

9 Aksakal, Mustafa (2008). *The Ottoman Road to War in 1914: The Ottoman Empire and the First World War*. Cambridge.

10 Bloxham, Donald (2002). 'The Beginning of the Armenian Catastrophe: Comparative and Contextual Considerations'. In: Hans-Lukas Kieser & Dominik J. Schaller (red.), *Der Völkermord an den Armeniern und die Shoah: The Armenian Genocide and the Shoah*. Zürich, pp. 101-28.

11 Akçam, Taner 'The Chilingirian Murder: A Case Study from the 1915 Roundup of Armenian Intellectuals'. In: *Holocaust and Genocide Studies*, Vol. 25, No. 1 (2011), pp. 127-44.

12 Derdarian, Mae M. (1996). *Vergeen: A Survivor of the Armenian Genocide*. Los Angeles, p. 38.

13 Dündar, Fuat (2008). *Modern Türkiye'nin Şifresi: İttihat ve Terakki'nin Etnisite Mühendisliği (1913-1918)*. Istanbul, pp. 248-348.

14 Kévorkian, Raymond H. (2011). *The Armenian Genocide: A Complete History*. London.

15 Sarafian, Ara (2001). 'The absorption of Armenian women and children into Muslim households as a structural component of the Armenian genocide'. In: Omer Bartov & Phyllis Mack (eds.), *In God's Name: Genocide and Religion in the Twentieth Century*. Oxford, pp. 209-21.

16 Bevan, Robert (2006). *The Destruction of Memory: Architecture at War*. London, pp. 25-60.

17 *Die Ziele und Taten armenischer Revolutionäre: The Armenian aspirations and revolutionary movements: Aspirations et mouvements révolutionaires arméniens: Ermeni Âmâl ve Harekât-ı İhtilâliyesi, Tesâvir ve Vesâik*. Istanbul, 1332.

18 Morgenthau, Henry (2000). *Ambassador Morgenthau's Story*. Princeton, pp. 224-5.

19 Andonian, Aram (1913). *Badgerazart Untartzag Badmootiun Balkanian Baderazmin*. Istanbul.

20 Weiss-Wendt, Anton & Uğur Ümit Üngör. 'Collaboration in Genocide', in: *Holocaust and Genocide Studies*, Vol. 25, No. 3 (2011).

21 *United States National Archives*, RG 59, 867.4016/67, 29 May 1915.

22 Sarafian, Ara (ed.) (2005). *The Treatment of Armenians in the Ottoman Empire 1915-16: Documents Presented to Viscount Grey of Fallodon by Viscount Bryce*. London.

23 Gust, Wolfgang (ed.) (2005). *Der Völkermord an den Armeniern 1915/16: Dokumente aus dem Politischen Archiv des deutschen Auswärtigen Amts*. Hamburg.

24 Winter, Jay (ed.) (2003). *America and the Armenian Genocide of 1915*. Cambridge.

25 Dadrian, Vahram (2003). *To the Desert: Pages from my Diary*. London.

26 Miller, Donald E. & Lorne Touryan-Miller (1993). *Survivors: An Oral History of the Armenian Genocide*. Berkeley, CA, p. 146.

27 *Takvim-i Vekâyi*, no.3540 (1919), p. 7.

28 Odian, Yervant (2009). *Accursed Years: My Exile and Return from Der Zor, 1914-1919*. London.

29 Dadrian, Vahakn N. & Taner Akçam (eds.) (2011). *Judgment at Istanbul: The Armenian Genocide Trials*. New York: Berghahn.

Youth unit working in the rice fields
Source: Documentation Center of Cambodia

The Cambodian Genocide, 1975-1979

Ben Kiernan

'In the years 1975 and 1976, they were killing people every day. Killings took place at some dis-tance from the village. I heard that victims were bound and then beaten to death. They were usually people found to be fishing illegally or who had failed to inform the Khmer Rouge of all their activities. Also during 1975-76, food was scarce in the village; rice porridge with banana stalks was the usual meal.'[1]

A 12 year old peasant boy, who was separated from his parents, in a later memory of the Khmer Rouge

Introduction

Khmer Rouge forces took over Cambodia on 17 April 1975. They forcibly evacuated the nation's cities, emptied hospitals and Buddhist monasteries, closed schools and factories, abolished money and wages, and scattered libraries. Freedom of the press, movement, worship, organisation, association, and discussion all disappeared for nearly four years. So did family life. Cambodians were forced to take their meals in collective mess halls. Parents ate in sittings; if they were lucky, their sons and daughters waited their turn outside. During the years 1975 to 1979, Democratic Kampuchea (DK) was a prison camp state. Its 8 million prisoners served most of their time in solitary confinement. 1.7 million inmates were worked, starved, or beaten to death.

1. The rise of the Khmer Rouge

Rural conditions were better in prerevolutionary Cambodia than in neighbouring countries like Vietnam or even Thailand. Land was more equitably distributed, and most peasant families owned some land. However, rural debt was common, and the number of landless tenants or sharecroppers increased from 4% of the farming population in 1950 to 20% in 1970.[2] Thus, alongside a landowning middle peasant class, a new class of rootless, destitute rural dwellers emerged. Their position was desperate enough for them to have little to lose in any kind of social revolution.

The gulf between town and countryside has been cited as a major factor in the Khmer Rouge's march to power. Unlike the countryside, the cities were not predominantly Khmer, but included large populations of ethnic Chinese and Vietnamese. Nor was the urban manufacturing sector very significant, producing few consumer goods for the countryside. Many peasants saw cities as seats of arbitrary, even foreign, political and economic power. But none of this, of course, explains why the Khmer Rouge regime also turned against the peasantry in such large numbers.

Another factor was the rapid expansion of education in Cambodia in the 1960s, following the long neglect of education under French colonial rule. A generation gap separated peasant parents from educated youth, who were often unable to find work after graduating from high school and so drifted into political dissidence. The Khmer Rouge in the 1960s recruited disproportionately among schoolteachers and students.

After completing a scholarship in France, Pol Pot — the future Khmer Rouge leader — returned to Cambodia in 1953. During the 1960s, he and other younger, mostly French-educated Cambodian communists took over the leadership of the more orthodox (pro-Vietnamese) Workers' Party of Kampuchea, which had led the independence struggle against French colonialism while they were back in Paris. In 1966, the new leadership changed the party's name to 'Communist Party of Kampuchea' (CPK) and set out on their path to power by staging an uprising against Prince Norodom Sihanouk's neutralist government.

The Sihanouk regime was increasingly repressive, which drove the grass-roots left into dissidence, enabling the French-educated Khmers of elite background, led by Pol Pot, to harness these home-grown veterans of the independence struggle to its plans for rebellion in 1967-1968. Conflict between the Vietnamese and Chinese Communists over Cambodia gave Pol Pot's faction Chinese support and valuable manoeuvrability against the orthodox pro-Vietnamese Khmer Communists.

Although it was an indigenous political phenomenon, Pol Pot's regime could not have come to power without the massive economic and military destabilisation of Cambodia by the United States, beginning in 1966. On 18 March 1969, the U.S. Air Force began a secret B-52 bombardment of Vietnamese sanctuaries in rural Cambodia.[3] Exactly one year later, Prince Norodom Sihanouk was overthrown by the U.S.-backed general, Lon Nol. The Vietnam War spilled across the Vietnam-Cambodia border, Sihanouk swore revenge, and a new civil war tore Cambodia apart.

The U.S. bombing of the countryside increased from 1970 until 15 August 1973, when the U.S. Congress imposed a halt. Up to 150,000 Cambodians had been killed in the American bombardments. Nearly half of the 540,000 tons of bombs fell in the last six-month period. Hundreds of thousands of peasants fled into the cities, to escape first the bombing and then the imposition of Khmer Rouge power. From the ashes of rural Cambodia arose the CPK regime, led by Pol Pot.

Pol Pot's forces had profited greatly from the U.S. bombardment. Contemporary U.S. government documents and peasant survivors reveal that the Khmer Rouge used the bombing's devastation and massacre of civilians as recruitment propaganda, and as an excuse for their brutal, radical policies and their purge of moderate and pro-Vietnamese Khmer Communists and Sihanoukists. They took national power in 1975 after defeating Sihanouk's successor regime, that of Marshal Lon Nol.

2. Organising the genocide

The CPK Centre, known as *Angkar Loeu* (the high organisation), began its purges in the 1960s by assassinating Party figures assumed to be too close to Vietnam's Communists. In the early 1970s, before taking power at the national level, the Centre arranged the arrest and 'disappearances' of nearly 900 Hanoi-trained Khmer Communists who had returned home from North Vietnam to join the insurgency against Lon Nol's regime. They accounted for half the Party's membership in 1970.

Democratic Kampuchea was initially divided into six major zones and 32 regions, each of which in turn comprised districts, subdistricts, and villages. One aim of the CPK Centre was to build larger and larger units at the local level, abolishing village life altogether in favour of 'high-level cooperatives' the size of a subdistrict. At the other end of the hierarchy, the Centre set about reducing the autonomy of the zones by bringing them under its own direct control.

Children at work during Democratic Kampuchea
Source: Documentation Center of Cambodia

'Then, from January 1977, all children over about eight years of age, including people of my age [20 years], were separated from their parents, whom we were no longer allowed to see although we remained in the village. We were divided into groups consisting of young men, young women, and young children, each group nominally 300-strong. The food, mostly rice and salt, was pooled and served communally. [...] Also in early 1977, collective marriages, involving hundreds of mostly unwilling couples, took place for the first time. All personal property was confiscated. A new round of executions began, more wide-ranging than that of 1975 and involving anyone who could not or would not carry out work directions. Food rations were cut significantly, leading to many more deaths from starvation, as were clothing allowances. Three sets of clothes per year was now the rule. Groups of more than two people were forbidden to assemble.'

Thoun Cheng (b. 1957), who fled the Pol Pot regime in 1977

The Centre gradually exerted totalitarian control over the population by replacing autonomous or dissident Zone administrations and Party Committees with Centre-backed forces commanded by loyalist Zone leaders Mok and Ke Pauk. By 1978, purges had taken the lives of half of the members of the Party's Central Committee, although there is no evidence that this body had ever officially met.

A common pattern was for Mok's or Pauk's forces to undermine a Zone from below, first purging the district and village committees, then the regional ones, before finally picking off the weakened Zone Party leadership. From 1973, with Centre backing, Mok had seized control of the Southwest Zone Party Committee, executing his senior and rival, Prasith, who had been number 7 in the 1963 Party hierarchy. Then after victory in 1975, Pauk's forces carried out a violent purge of cadres loyal to his executed predecessor, Koy Thuon, in the Northern Zone, renamed the Central Zone. In 1977, Mok's Southwest Zone forces and administrators carried out a similar purge of the Northwest Zone.

Those arrested were taken to the nerve centre of the system, the national security service (santebal) prison in Phnom Penh, code-named Office S-21, preserved today as the Tuol Sleng Museum of Genocide. Up to 20,000 people, mostly suspected CPK dissidents and regional officials, were tortured and killed there from 1976 to 1979. Chief of the santebal, Kaing Khek Iev, alias Deuch, reported directly to Son Sen, the Centre official responsible for security.

3. The ideology of genocide

Along with Stalinist and Maoist models, an underlying theme of the political worldview of the Pol Pot group was a concern for national and racial grandiosity. Their disagreements with Vietnamese Communists in Paris in the early 1950s concerned the symbolic grandeur of the medieval Khmer temple of Angkor Wat and their sensitivities over the small size of Cambodia's population. In their view, Cambodia did not need to learn or import anything from its neighbours. Rather, they would recover its pre-Buddhist glory by rebuilding the powerful economy of the medieval Angkor kingdom and regain 'lost territory' from Vietnam and Thailand. Democratic Kampuchea treasured the Cambodian 'race', not individuals. National impurities included the foreign-educated (except for Pol Pot's Paris-educated group) and 'hereditary enemies', especially Vietnamese. To return Cambodians to their imagined origins, the Pol Pot group saw the need for war, and for 'secrecy as the basis' of the revolution.[4] Few of the grass-roots, pragmatic Cambodian Communists could be trusted to implement such plans, which Pol Pot kept secret from them.

DK sealed Cambodia off from the world. The borders were closed, all neighbouring countries subject to military attack, the use of foreign languages was banned, embassies and press agencies were expelled, local newspapers and television shut down, radios and bicycles confiscated, mail and telephone communication suppressed. Cambodians soon learned that any display of knowledge or skill, if 'contaminated' by foreign influence, was dangerous. Human communications were reduced to daily instructions and orders.

The Party Centre, with its elite, urban background, French education, and a racial chauvinism little different from that of its predecessor (the Lon Nol regime), inhabited a different ideological world from that of the more moderate, Buddhist-educated, Vietnamese-trained peasant cadres who had made up the mass of the Party's membership. The acknowledged lack of a political base for its programme meant that it considered tactics of 'secrecy' and violence necessary. These were used first against suspected Party dissidents, then against the people of Cambodia as a whole (and especially ethnic minorities like the Vietnamese). Given the sacrifices from the population that the nationalist revival required, the resistance it naturally provoked, and the regime's preparedness to forge ahead 'at all costs', mass murder and genocide were the results.

> 'Also from 1975, money was abolished and big houses were either demolished, and the materials used for smaller ones, or used for administration or to house troops. The banana trees in the chamcar were all uprooted on the orders of the Khmer Rouge and rice planted in their place. Production was high, although some land was left fallow and rations usually just consisted of rice porridge with very little meat. After the harvest each year, trucks would come at night to take away the village's rice stores to an unknown destination.
>
> In 1975, the Khmer Rouge also began executing rich people, although they spared the elderly owner of 800 hectares. They also executed college students and former government officials, soldiers and police. I saw the bodies of many such people not far from the village.'
>
> Thoun Cheng (b. 1957), who fled the Pol Pot regime in 1977

4. Perpetrators

The DK ruling body was the Standing Committee of the Central Committee of the CPK. The leaders with maximum national power and responsibility for the mass murders and genocide about to be perpetrated were based in the capital, Phnom Penh, and were known as the 'Party Centre'. This small group of mostly post-1960 party leaders held national power and were responsible for initiating the genocidal policies.

> **Khmer Rouge Leaders**
>
> No. 1 — Saloth Sar (Pol Pot), Secretary-General of the CPK from 1962, and Prime Minister of DK;
>
> No. 2 — Nuon Chea, Deputy Secretary-General of the Party from 1960;
>
> No. 3 — Ieng Sary, ranked number 3 in the Party leadership from 1963 and one of DK's deputy prime ministers (responsible for Foreign Affairs);
>
> No. 11 — Son Sen, Deputy Prime Minister of DK (responsible for defence and security);
>
> Khieu Samphan, a Party member since the 1950s who became DK's president;
>
> Ieng Thirith, wife of Ieng Sary and DK Minister of Social Action;
>
> Yun Yat, wife of Son Sen and DK Minister of Culture.
>
> Two other figures who held regional posts in 1975 increasingly assumed responsibility for the implementation of genocidal policies throughout the country: Chhit Choeun, alias

Democratic Kampuchea leaders and members of the Standing Committee of the Central Committee of the CPK
Source: Documentation Center of Cambodia

> Mok, was CPK secretary of the key Southwest Zone and later Chief of the General Staff of the Khmer Rouge armed forces; and Ke Pauk, Party Secretary of the Central Zone of DK, later became Under Secretary-General of the Khmer Rouge armed forces.

The shadowy DK leaders gave few clues to their personal lives. In 1978, the first journalists into DK, from Yugoslavia, had to ask its Prime Minister, 'Who are you, comrade Pol Pot?'.[5] He never admitted that his real name was Saloth Sar. As a Cambodian student activist in Paris in 1952, he had stood out in his choice of a different *nom de plume:* the 'Original Cambodian' *(khmaer da'em).* Fellow students preferred less racial, modernist code-names, like 'Free Khmer' or 'Khmer Worker'.

5. Victims

5.1 Genocide against a religious group

Pol Pot's government tried to eradicate Buddhism from Cambodia. Eyewitnesses testify to the Khmer Rouge massacres of monks and the forcible disrobing and persecution of survivors. Out of a total of 2,680 Buddhist monks from eight of Cambodia's 3,000 monasteries, only 70 monks were found to have survived in 1979.[6] There is no reason to believe these eight monasteries were atypical. If the same death toll applied to the monks from all the other monasteries, fewer than 2,000 of Cambodia's 70,000 monks could be said to have survived.

Pol Pot, 1978
Source: Documentation Center of Cambodia. Photo: Elizabeth Becker

'Monks have disappeared from 90 to 95 per cent.... Monasteries... are largely abandoned. The foundation pillars of Buddhism... have disintegrated. In the future they will dissolve further. The political base, the economic base, the cultural base must be uprooted.'[7]
A CPK Centre document dated September 1975

Buddhism was eradicated from the face of the country in just one year; by early 1977, there were no functioning monasteries and no monks to be seen anywhere in Cambodia.

5.2   Genocide against ethnic groups

The largest ethnic minority groups in Cambodia before 1970 were the Vietnamese, the Chinese, and the Muslim Cham. Unlike most other Communist regimes, the Pol Pot regime's view of these and the country's 20 other national minorities, who had long made up over 15% of the Cambodian population, was virtually to deny their existence. The regime officially proclaimed that they totalled only 1% of the population. Statistically, they were written off.

Their physical fate was much worse. The Vietnamese community, for example, was en-

Ethnic people at the market, selling fabrics
Source: Documentation Center of Cambodia.

tirely eradicated. About half of the 450,000-strong community had been expelled by the United States-backed Lon Nol regime in 1970 (with several thousands killed in massacres). Over 100,000 more were driven out by the Pol Pot regime in the first year after its victory in 1975. The ones who remained in Cambodia were simply murdered.

In research conducted in Cambodia since 1979 it has not been possible to find a Vietnamese resident who had survived the Pol Pot years there. However, eyewitnesses from other ethnic groups, including Khmers who were married to Vietnamese, testify to the fates of their Vietnamese spouses and neighbours. What they witnessed was a campaign of systematic racial extermination.[8]

The Chinese under Pol Pot's regime suffered the worst disaster ever to befall any ethnic Chinese community in Southeast Asia. Of the 1975 population of 425,000, only 200,000 Chinese survived the next four years. Ethnic Chinese were nearly all urban, and they were seen by the Khmer Rouge as archetypal city dwellers, and as prisoners of war. In this case, they were not targeted for execution because of their race, but like other evacuated city dwellers they were made to work harder and under much more deplorable conditions than rural dwellers. The penalty for infraction of minor regulations was often death. This basically constituted systematic discrimination predicated on geographic or social origin.

The Chinese succumbed in particularly large numbers to hunger and to diseases like malaria. The 50% of them who perished is a higher proportion even than that estimated for Cambodia's city dwellers in general (about one-third).

Furthermore, the Chinese language, like all foreign and minority languages, was banned, and so was any tolerance of a culturally and ethnically distinguishable Chinese community. This, in essence, constituted being destroyed 'as such'.

The Muslim Chams numbered at least 250,000 in 1975. Their distinct religion, language and culture, large villages, and autonomous networks threatened the atomised, closely supervised society that the Pol Pot leadership planned. An early 1974 Pol Pot document records the decision to 'break up' the Cham people, adding: 'Do not allow too many of them to concentrate in one area'. Cham women were forced to cut their hair short in the Khmer style, not wear it long as was their custom; then the traditional Cham sarong was banned, as peasants were forced to wear only black pyjamas. Ultimately, restrictions were placed upon religious activity.

> 'Our Cham leaders were dismissed in 1976, and replaced by Khmers. We were not allowed to speak Cham. Only the Khmer language was allowed. From 1977, they said: "There are no Vietnamese, Chinese, Javanese [Chams and Malays] — only the Khmer race. Everyone is the same."'
>
> Nao Gha, a minority Cham Muslim woman

In 1975, the new Pol Pot government turned its attention to the Chams with a vengeance. Fierce rebellions broke out. On an island in the Mekong River, the authorities attempted to collect all copies of the Koran. The villagers staged a protest demonstration, and Khmer Rouge troops fired into the crowd. The Chams then took up swords and knives and slaughtered half a dozen troops. The retaliating armed forces massacred many and pillaged their homes. They evacuated the island, and razed the village, and then turned to a neighbouring village, massacring 70% of its inhabitants.

Soon after, the Pol Pot army forcibly emptied all 113 Cham villages in the country. About 100,000 Chams were massacred and the survivors were dispersed in small groups of several families. Islamic schools and religion, as well as the Cham language, were banned. Thousands of Muslims were physically forced to eat pork. Many were murdered for refusing. Of 113 Cham *hakkem,* or community leaders, only 20 survived in 1979. Only 25 of their 226 deputies survived. All but 38 of about 300 religious teachers at Cambodia's Koranic schools perished. Of more than a thousand who had made the pilgrimage to Mecca, only about 30 survived.[9]

The toll goes on. The Thai minority of 20,000 was reportedly reduced to about 8,000. Of the 1,800 families of the Lao ethnic minority, only 800 families survived. Of the 2,000 members of the Kola minority, 'no trace... has been found'.[10]

Photographs of victims that were imprisoned at S-21
Source: Documentation Center of Cambodia

5.3 Genocide against a part of the majority national group

Finally, of the majority Khmers, 15 percent of the rural population perished between 1975 and 1979, and 25% of the urban population (see Table 1). Democratic Kampuchea initially divided its population into the 'old citizens' (those who had lived in Khmer Rouge Zones before 1975) and 'new citizens' (those who had lived in the cities, the last holdouts of the Lon Nol regime). All cities were evacuated in April 1975.

'The Khmer Rouge victory in April 1975 and their evacuation of Phnom Penh city brought 600 more people to Banteay Chey. The newcomers were billeted with village families. Relatives of ours, a couple and their three children, and one single man, stayed in my father's house. They had set out on foot from Phnom Penh 15 days earlier and arrived tired and hungry, although unlike some others they had not lost any of their family members along the way. [...] In return for food and shelter, the new arrivals in Banteay Chey helped the locals in their work in the fields. Also in April 1975, Khmer Rouge troops came to live in the village. It was not long before they began imposing a very harsh lifestyle on the villagers. Everybody was now obliged to work in the fields or dig reservoirs from 3 or 4 AM until 10 PM.'

Thoun Cheng (b. 1957), who fled the Pol Pot regime in 1977

In 1976, however, the 'new citizens' were redesignated as 'deportees', and most failed to even qualify for the next category, 'candidates', let alone 'full rights citizens', a group to which only favoured peasant families were admitted. But not even they were spared the mass murders of the 1977-1978 nationwide purges.

The most horrific slaughter was perpetrated in the last six months of the regime, in the politically suspect Eastern Zone bordering Vietnam. After the Khmer Rouge killed hundreds in mass executions, tens of thousands of other villagers were deported to the northwest of the country. En route through Phnom Penh they were 'marked' as easterners by being forced to wear a blue scarf, reminiscent of Hitler's yellow star for Jews,[11] and later eliminated en masse. A total 1978 murder toll of over 100,000 (more than one-seventeenth of the eastern population) can safely be regarded as a minimum estimate.[12] The real figure is probably much higher (Table 1).

TABLE 1 Approximate Death Tolls under Pol Pot, 1975-1979

Social group	1975 pop.	Numbers perished	%
'New Citizens'			
Urban Khmer	2,000,000	500,000	25
Rural Khmer	600,000	150,000	25
Chinese (all urban)	430,000	215,000	50
Vietnamese (urban)	10,000	10,000	100
Lao (rural)	10,000	4,000	40
TOTAL New citizens	3,050,000	879,000	29
'Base Citizens'			
Rural Khmer	4,500,000	675,000	15
Khmer Krom	5,000	2,000	40
Cham (all rural)	250,000	90,000	36
Vietnamese (rural)	10,000	10,000	100
Thai (rural)	20,000	8,000	40
Upland minorities	60,000	9,000	15
TOTAL Base citizens	4,840,000	792,000	16
Cambodia	7,890,000	1,671,000	21

6. The long-term impact on the victim groups

In 1979 the population of Cambodia totalled around 6.5 million. The survivors thus emerged from the Pol Pot period nearly 3.5 million fewer than the 1980 population that had been pro-jected in 1970.[13] Not all of the difference is attributable to the Pol Pot regime; much is the result of the American war and aerial bombardment of the populated areas of Cambodia from

Cambodians rejoicing after liberation, January 17, 1979
Source: Documentation Center of Cambodia

1969-1973, and of projected population growth that was unrealised due to instability, population displacement, and harsh living conditions throughout the 1970s. But 1.7 million deaths are directly attributable to the Khmer Rouge regime.

The Cambodian population was severely affected by psychological trauma. Post-traumatic stress syndrome became a general problem, including illnesses such as psychosomatic blindness, which has been diagnosed among survivors living in the United States.

7. International responses

In January 1979, the Vietnamese army invaded Cambodia, driving out the Khmer Rouge. A much less repressive regime was established with Hun Sen, first as Foreign Minister, and then as Prime Minister from 1985 onward. Vietnamese troops withdrew in 1989, after training a new Cambodian army that succeeded in defending the country on its own. But most of the international community embargoed the new government and continued to recognise the 'legitimacy' of the defunct Pol Pot regime, voting for it to occupy Cambodia's UN seat for another 12 years. Therefore, until 1989, the Khmer Rouge flag flew over New York, and until 1992 Pol Pot's ambassador ran Cambodia's mission there. No Western country voted against the right of the government-in-exile dominated by the Khmer Rouge to represent their former victims in international forums.[16] Most Western governments instead portrayed the Vietnamese invasion as the cause of the 'Cambodian problem'.

International loyalty persists

While the Cambodian genocide progressed, Washington, Beijing, and Bangkok all supported the continued independent existence of the Khmer Rouge regime. The U.S. Secretary of State Henry Kissinger tells the foreign minister of neighbouring Thailand, on 26 November, 1975:

'You should also tell the Cambodians that we will be friends with them. They are murderous thugs, but we won't let that stand in our way. We are prepared to improve relations with them.'[14]

Two weeks later, Kissinger and U.S. President Gerald Ford visited Southeast Asia. Ford told Indonesia's President Suharto: 'The unification of Vietnam has come more quickly than we anticipated. There is, however, resistance in Cambodia to the influence of Hanoi. We are willing to move slowly in our relations with Cambodia, hoping perhaps to slow down the North Vietnamese influence although we find the Cambodian government very difficult.' Kissinger then explained Beijing's similar strategy: 'The Chinese want to use Cambodia to balance off Vietnam. We don't like Cambodia, for the government in many ways is worse than Vietnam, but we would like it to be independent. We don't discourage Thailand or China from drawing closer to Cambodia'.[15]

In the decade following Pol Pot's overthrow, many reputable legal organisations dismissed proposals to send delegations to Cambodia to investigate the crimes of the DK regime. They all refused such opportunities to report on what the UN's Special Rapporteur on genocide, Benjamin Whitaker, described in 1985 as genocide, 'even under the most restricted definition'.

A few voluntary organisations around the world pressed on, unaided by major human rights groups. These included the U.S. Cambodia Genocide Project, which in 1980 proposed a World Court case; the Australian section of the International Commission of Jurists, which in January 1990 called for 'international trials' of the Pol Pot leadership for genocide; the Minnesota Lawyers International Human Rights Committee, which in June 1990 organised a one-day mock trial of the Khmer Rouge following the procedures of the World Court, with testimony by a dozen victims of the genocide; the Washington-based Campaign to Oppose the Return of the Khmer Rouge, supported by 45 U.S. organisations, a former Cambodian Prime Minister, and survivors of the Khmer Rouge period; Yale University's Cambodian Genocide Programme; and the NGO Forum, an international body of private voluntary agencies working in Cambodia.

8. The road to justice

Finally in the early 1990s, public pressure on governments mounted in Western countries. The UN Subcommission on Human Rights, which the previous year had quietly dropped from its agenda a draft resolution condemning the Pol Pot genocide, now passed a resolution noting 'the duty of the international community to prevent the recurrence of genocide in Cambodia' and 'to take all necessary preventive measures to avoid conditions that could create for the Cambodian people the risk of new crimes against humanity' (UN Subcommission on Human Rights, 1991). For the first time, the genocide was acknowledged in an official international arena. *The New York Times* called on Washington to publish its 'list of Khmer Rouge war criminals and insist on their exclusion from Cambodian political life', and for their trial before 'an international tribunal for crimes against humanity'.

In Paris on 23 October 1991, as the Paris Peace Agreement was signed, U.S. Secretary of State James Baker stated: 'Cambodia and the U.S. are both signatories to the Genocide Convention and we will support efforts to bring to justice those responsible for the mass murders of the 1970s if the new Cambodian government chooses to pursue this path'.[17]

In October 1991, U.S. Assistant Secretary of State Richard Solomon said Washington 'would be absolutely delighted to see Pol Pot and the others brought to justice for the unspeakable violence of the 1970s'. He blamed Hun Sen for the Paris Agreement's failure that year to include provision for a trial: 'Mr. Hun Sen had promoted the idea over the summer months of a tribunal to deal with this issue. For reasons that he would have to explain he dropped that idea at the end of the negotiations'. The facts show, however, that the United States had not supported the idea of a trial from the time it was broached in June 1986 by Australia's Foreign Minister Bill Hayden, and that it was the United States and China that had forced Hun Sen to drop the demand.[18]

The struggle to bring the Khmer Rouge leaders to justice began to bear fruit after the 1993 UN-sponsored elections, when the Khmer Rouge killed peacekeepers from Bangladesh, Bulgaria, Japan, and China. Following the UN's withdrawal, in 1994, the new Cambodian coalition government outlawed the Khmer Rouge insurgency, which began to fragment. Treason and paranoia led to the final downfall of the Khmer Rouge leaders. In June 1997, fearing further betrayal, Pol Pot murdered Son Sen. In the jungle of northern Cambodia, as the last military forces loyal to Pol Pot abandoned their base, they drove their trucks over the bodies of their final victims: Son Sen, his wife Yun Yat — the DK Minister of Culture — and a dozen of their family members. Mok turned in pursuit, arrested Pol Pot, and subjected him to a show trial in the jungle for the murder of Son Sen. But in March 1998, former Deputy Commander Ke Pauk led a new mutiny against Mok, and also defected to the government. The next month, as the various factions slugged it out, Pol Pot died in his sleep.

In December 1998, the top surviving Khmer Rouge leaders — Nuon Chea, former Deputy Party Secretary, and Khieu Samphan, former DK Head of State — surrendered to the government. Cambodian troops captured Mok in March 1999. And the next month, Kang Khek Iev, alias Deuch, the former commandant of Tuol Sleng prison, was discovered by a British journalist. He, too, was quickly arrested by Hun Sen's police. Phnom Penh prosecutors announced that Deuch and Mok would be charged with genocide, and that both Nuon Chea and Khieu Samphan would be summoned to testify and would also be charged with genocide. Despite the deaths of Son Sen, Pol Pot, Ke Pauk (who died in 2002), and Mok (2006), five or more DK leaders remain liable to prosecution.

7.1 The ECCC

Cambodia's two Prime Ministers, Hun Sen and King Sihanouk's son Norodom Ranariddh, had appealed in 1997 to the UN to establish an international tribunal to judge the crimes of the Khmer Rouge. In response, the UN created a Group of Experts to examine the evidence, including the documents collected by Yale's Cambodian Genocide Programme and its now-independent offshoot, the Documentation Centre of Cambodia. The UN experts concluded in 1999 that the Khmer Rouge should face charges 'for crimes against humanity and genocide'. They reported that the events of 1975-1979 fit the definition of the crime outlawed by the United Nations Genocide Convention of 1948. In their view, the Khmer Rouge regime had 'subjected the people of Cambodia to almost all of the acts enumerated in the Convention. The more difficult task is determining whether the Khmer Rouge carried out these acts with the requisite intent and against groups protected by the Convention.' The experts' response to this challenge was affirmative.

Khmer Rouge leader Deuch sentenced by ECCC, 26 July 2010
Source: United Nations

Intent — Could 'genocidal intent' be proved in the case of Cambodia?
UN Experts: 'In the view of the group of experts, the existing historical research justifies including genocide within the jurisdiction of a tribunal to prosecute Khmer Rouge leaders. In particular, evidence suggests the need for prosecutors to investigate the commission of genocide against the Cham, Vietnamese and other minority groups, and the Buddhist monkhood. The Khmer Rouge subjected these groups to an especially harsh and extensive measure of the acts enumerated in the Convention. The requisite intent has support in direct and indirect evidence, including Khmer Rouge statements, eyewitness accounts, and the nature and numbers of victims in each group, both in absolute terms and in proportion to each group's total population. These groups qualify as protected groups under the Convention: the Muslim Cham as an ethnic and religious group; the Vietnamese communities as an ethnic and, perhaps, a racial group; and the Buddhist monkhood as a religious group.'
'Specifically, in the case of the Buddhist monkhood, their intent is evidenced by the Khmer Rouge's intensely hostile statements towards religion, and the monkhood in par-

ticular; the Khmer Rouge's policies to eradicate the physical and ritualistic aspects of the Buddhist religion; the disrobing of monks and abolition of the monkhood; the number of victims; and the executions of Buddhist leaders and recalcitrant monks. Likewise, in addition to the number of victims, the intent to destroy the Cham and other ethnic minorities appears evidenced by such Khmer Rouge actions as their announced policy of homogenisation, the total prohibition of these groups' distinctive cultural traits, their dispersal among the general population, and the execution of their leadership.'

From 1999 to 2006, the UN negotiated with the Cambodian government and established a joint tribunal in Phnom Penh to ensure legal accountability for the Khmer Rouge's crimes. In 2007, the Cambodian and international co-prosecutors of the new Extraordinary Chambers in the Courts of Cambodia (ECCC) alleged that the defunct CPK regime had committed 'crimes against humanity [and] genocide'. The ECCC assumed custody of the imprisoned S-21 commander Deuch, and also jailed, pending trial, four surviving leaders of the CPK 'Party Centre': Nuon Chea, Khieu Samphan, Ieng Sary, and Ieng Thirith. After Deuch's 2009 trial for crimes against humanity, the ECCC announced that the other four defendants would face the additional charge of genocide for Khmer Rouge crimes against Cambodia's Cham and Vietnamese minorities. Their trial began in mid-2011.

This chapter is an abbreviated version of a chapter that was previously published in Samuel Totten (ed.): *Century of Genocide*, with permission of the publisher and author.

Chhit Choeun, alias Mok (1925-2006)
Member of the CPK CC from 1963. With Ke Pauk, he was one of
one of Pol Pot's two principal military supporters. In 1997 he
rebelled against Pol's leadership.

Deuch, alias Kaing Khek Iev, Duch (b. 1942)
Director of S-21 from 1975-1979, the national security service *(santebal)* prison in Phnom Penh preserved today as the Tuol Sleng
Museum of Genocide. After the fall of Democratic Kampuchea,
he worked in Beijing for Radio China International.

Lon Nol (1913-1985)
Under Sihanouk Nol was Defence Minister and Chief of the
General Staff. In March 1970 he overthrew Sihanouk in a coup
d'état. Six months later he became President of the republic of
Cambodia. In April 1975 he fled to Hawaii.

Saloth Sar, alias Pol Pot (1928-1998)
The Khmer Rouge leader. Pot is often seen as the personification
of the regime and bearing the greatest responsibility. After the
Vietnamese invaded Cambodia he fled to the jungle, where he
died in 1998.

Hun Sen (b. 1952)
Sen was deputy Khmer Rouge regimental commander. After the
Vietnamese invasion he became Minister of Foreign Affairs in
the Vietnamese-installed Cambodian government, 1979-1986.
Currently he is Prime Minister of Cambodia.

Son Sen, alias Khieu, Khamm, Aum (1927-1997)
Sen was Chief of the General Staff of the Khmer Rouge Army and
Minister of Defence from August 1975. He was responsible for the
Tuol Sleng interrogation centre. In June 1997, fearing betrayal,
Pol Pot ordered his murder.

Norodom Sihanouk (b. 1922)

Sihanouk was King of Cambodia from 1941-1955 and Head of State from 1960-1970. Overthrown by Lon Nol in a coup in d'état in March 1970. He opened the way to the Paris Peace Agreement of 1991 by renewing his alliance with the Khmer Rouges in 1982. Became King of Cambodia for the second time in 1993.

Ke Vin, alias Ke Pauk (1933-2002)

Ke Pauk was CPK Secretary of the Northern Zone. He was one of Pol Pot's two principal military supporters.

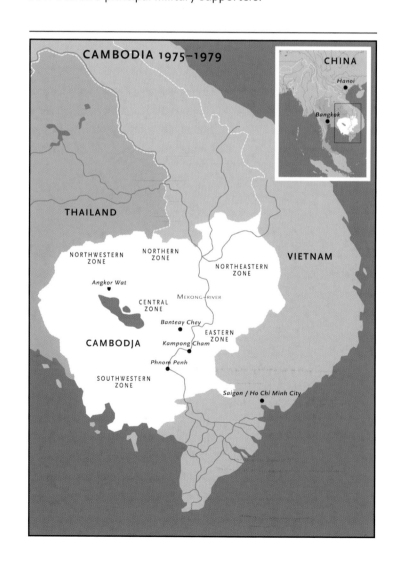

Angkar	The 'Organisation' (Communist Party of Kampuchea).
Angkar Loeu	The Higher Organisation (the Communist Party of Kampuchea Centre).
CPK	Communist Party of Kampuchea.
DK	Democratic Kampuchea, Cambodia under Khmer Rouge regime, from 1975 to 1979 a prison camp state.
ECCC	Extraordinary Chambers in the Courts of Cambodia.
Full right citizens	A group to which only favoured peasant families were admitted.
Khmaer da'em	Original Khmer or Cambodian.
Khmer Rouge	Pol Pot's regime that took over Cambodia on 17 April 1975.
New Citizens	Those who had lived in the cities, the last holdouts of the Lon Nol regime. In 1976, however, the 'new citizens' were redesignated 'deportees'.
Office S-21	The national security service *(santebal)* prison in Phnom Penh, preserved today as the Tuol Sleng Museum of Genocide.
Old Citizens	Those who had lived in Khmer Rouge Zones before 1975.
Santebal	DK Ministry of Security, the national security service.

Timeline

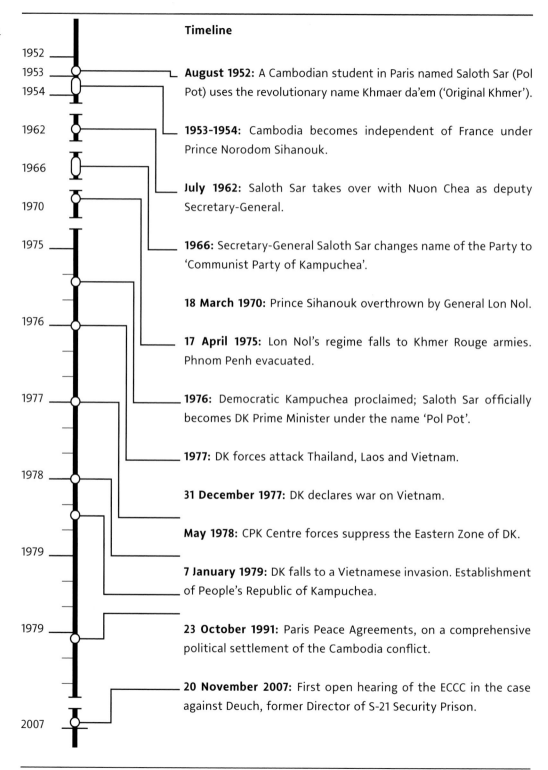

1952
1953
1954

1962

1966

1970

1975

1976

1977

1978

1979

1979

2007

August 1952: A Cambodian student in Paris named Saloth Sar (Pol Pot) uses the revolutionary name Khmaer da'em ('Original Khmer').

1953-1954: Cambodia becomes independent of France under Prince Norodom Sihanouk.

July 1962: Saloth Sar takes over with Nuon Chea as deputy Secretary-General.

1966: Secretary-General Saloth Sar changes name of the Party to 'Communist Party of Kampuchea'.

18 March 1970: Prince Sihanouk overthrown by General Lon Nol.

17 April 1975: Lon Nol's regime falls to Khmer Rouge armies. Phnom Penh evacuated.

1976: Democratic Kampuchea proclaimed; Saloth Sar officially becomes DK Prime Minister under the name 'Pol Pot'.

1977: DK forces attack Thailand, Laos and Vietnam.

31 December 1977: DK declares war on Vietnam.

May 1978: CPK Centre forces suppress the Eastern Zone of DK.

7 January 1979: DK falls to a Vietnamese invasion. Establishment of People's Republic of Kampuchea.

23 October 1991: Paris Peace Agreements, on a comprehensive political settlement of the Cambodia conflict.

20 November 2007: First open hearing of the ECCC in the case against Deuch, former Director of S-21 Security Prison.

Notes

1   All quotes come from testimonies collected by Ben Kiernan and Chanthou Boua in 1979 and 1980, published in Totten, *Century of Genocide*.

2   Kiernan, Ben, and Chanthou, Boua (Eds.) (1982). *Peasants and Politics in Kampuchea, 1942-1981*. London, p. 4.

3   Shawcross, William (1979). *Sideshow: Kissinger, Nixon and the Destruction of Cambodia*. New York, pp. 21-23, 31.

4   Boua, Chanthou' Chandler, David P., and Kiernan, Ben (Eds.) (1988). *Pol Pot Plans the Future: Confidential Leadership Documents from Democratic Kampuchea, 1976-77*. New Haven, CT: Yale Council on Southeast Asia Studies, pp. 214, 220.

5   Pol Pot (1978). *Interview of Comrade Pol Pot... to the Delegation of Yugoslav Journalists in Visit to Democratic Kampuchea. March 23*. Phnom Penh: Democratic Kampuchea, Ministry of Foreign Affairs, pp. 20-21.

6   Boua, Chanthou (1991). 'Genocide of a Religious Group: Pol Pot and Cambodia's Buddhist Monks', pp. 227-40. In P.T. Bushnell, V. Schlapentokh, C. Vanderpool, and J. Sundram (Eds.). *State-Organized Terror: The Case of Violent Internal Repression*. Boulder, CO, p. 239.

7   Boua, 1991, p. 235.

8   Kiernan, Ben (2008). *Genocide and Resistance in Southeast Asia: Documentation, Denial, and Justice in Cambodia and East Timor*. New Brunswick, NJ, pp. 296-98, 393-94, 423-27.

9   Kiernan, Ben (1988). 'Orphans of Genocide: The Cham Muslims of Kampuchea under Pol Pot'. *Bulletin of Concerned Asian Scholars*, 20(4):2-33.

10   Kiernan, Ben (1990). 'The Survival of Cambodia's Ethnic Minorities'. *Cultural Survival*, 14(3):64-66.

11   Kiernan, Ben (1989). 'Blue Scarf/Yellow Star: A Lesson in Genocide'. *Boston Globe*, February 27, p. 13.

12   Kiernan, Ben (1986). *Cambodia: Eastern Zone Massacres*. New York: Columbia University, Centre for the Study of Human Rights, Documentation Series No. 1.

13   Migozzi, Jacques (1973). *Cambodge: faits et problémes de population*. Paris: Centre National de la Recherche Scientifique, p. 269.

14   Kiernan 2008, p.1.

15   Burr, W., and Evans, M.L. (Eds.) (2001). 'Text of Ford-Kissinger-Suharto Discussion, U.S. Embassy Jakarta Telegram 1579 to Secretary State, December 6, 1975'. In *East Timor Revisited: Ford, Kissinger and the Indonesian Invasion, 1975-76*. Washington: National Security Archive.

16   Ibid.

17   Shenon, Philip (1991). 'Cambodian Factions Sign Peace Pact'. October 24, *New York Times*, p. A16.

18   Kiernan, Ben (1991). 'Deferring Peace in Cambodia: Regional Rapprochement, Superpower Obstruction', pp. 59-82. In George W.Breslauer, Harry Kreisler, and Benjamin Ward (Eds.). *Beyond the Cold War*. Berkeley: Institute of International Studies, University of California.

19   Short, P. (2005). *Pol Pot: Anatomy of a nightmare*. London.

'Windows of Hope', Kigali Genocide Memorial Centre
Photo: Thijs B. Bouwknegt

The Rwandan Genocide, 1994

Maria van Haperen

'After the aeroplane crashed, we no longer asked ourselves who supported the programme of the president's party or that of an opposition party. We only thought about one thing.
Questions were no longer asked about who was used to handling guns, who had experience with this or that militia, or who had never let a machete fall from their hands. There was work to be done, and you did it as well as you could. Nobody cared about whether someone would have preferred to listen to the mayor's commands or to those of the Interahamwe, or had followed the orders given by our municipal councillor, whom we knew well. You obeyed everyone and that was that. All of a sudden, Hutus became patriotic brothers, and there were no political differences of opinion between them. We assembled on the football field in a trusted group and set off together, united in our hunt.'[1]
Pancrace Hakizamungili, one of the many Hutus who took part in the genocide

'When Habyarimana's aeroplane was shot down on 6 April 1994, we were all at home. We saw many people running in all directions. When the perpetrators started burning people's houses, we ran to the parish church. On Friday 15 April, the Interahamwe surrounded it. Mayor Gacumbitsi was with the soldiers. He told them, "Take your tools and get to work. You hit snakes on the head to kill them." They started killing… I lay among the corpses and tried to hold my breath. They would throw rocks or pick up kids and throw them in the air. They threw a stone at me and I screamed for mercy, but one of our neighbours, Pascal, said, "I recognise that brat. Isn't she from Bikoramuki's family? All the rest of her family is dead, so what's so tough about her that we can't manage her?" He kicked me and spat on the ground saying that he wouldn't splash my blood onto him. Then he cut my head with a machete. I don't know what happened after that.'[2]
Valentine Iribagiza, survivor Rwandan genocide

Introduction

The 1994 Rwanda genocide was the result of an economic crisis, civil war, population growth and a struggle for state power. The president of Rwanda at the time, Juvénal Habyarimana, had decided, after long opposition, to comply with the Arusha Accords and put an end to the crisis and civil war. The civil war began when the armed wing of the Rwandan Patriotic Front (RPF) invaded from Uganda in the autumn of 1990. The RPF was a movement mainly made up of the Tutsi refugee diaspora in Uganda with which Habyarimana's party, the National Revolutionary Movement for Development (MRND), had been forced to compromise. On 6 April, he flew back from negotiations in the Tanzanian capital, Dar es Salaam. His aeroplane was shot down as it came into land, and the president and a number of other top officials were killed. After the announcement of the death of the president, all hell broke loose in Rwanda. A group of senior military officials quickly seized power. Almost immediately, organised massacres of Tutsi and moderate Hutu began, initiated by the army and the Interahamwe and Impuzamugambi youth militia.

It was not immediately clear what exactly was happening. The images on the news showed long queues of people fleeing the country, carrying their household effects. Young shabbily dressed men called heatedly for 'Hutu power,' waving machetes or holding huge weapons aloft and firing into the air. Piles of corpses lay along the sides of roads and in ditches, but there was a lack of clarity in the media's observations and analyses. People spoke of the Hutu and the Tutsi, and by referring to the chaos as an intertribal dispute, US President Bill Clinton confirmed people's prejudices about Africa.

1. Historical background

Rwanda is situated in the Central African Great Lakes Region, close to the equator. It is not a large country; it is around 10% smaller than Belgium. Rwanda is a lush country, covered in numerous hills. It is quite fertile by African standards, and there are many swamps, lakes and rivers.

Centuries ago three peoples settled in the area that comprises present-day Rwanda and Burundi: the baTwa in the 6th century, followed by the baHutu in the 7th century, and the baTutsi[3] in the course of the 8th and 9th centuries. The majority of the population made a living out of agriculture: the Hutu were predominantly crop cultivators and came from the North West. The Tutsi were cattle farmers and came from the regions to the south and east of Lake Victoria (Tanzania). The Twa were a pygmy people who made a living from hunting, gathering and pottery-making. The Twa lived in the forest-covered mountains, isolated from the Hutu and Tutsi. Many Tutsi travelled through the area with large herds. As agriculturalists, the Hutu lived in permanent settlements.

1.1 Early power structures

Both the Hutu and the Tutsi lived in clans that had their own leaders. The power structures within these clans were hierarchical; the people were subservient to their clan leaders. Initially, the possession of cattle conferred status. In the 19th century, agricultural land and armies also increasingly contributed to a clan leader's power. Clan leaders showed loyalty to the king, the *mwami,* who came from the Tutsi community. While an absolute monarchy did not develop, a centralised society with socially distinct communities did evolve in Rwanda. However, clan leaders maintained a degree of autonomy within the system.

At the end of the 19th century social status became increasingly linked to being 'Hutu' or 'Tutsi'. The Hutu were generally seen as 'the masses', because few people owned cattle. In the course of time, a Hutu who obtained cattle would be seen as a Tutsi. If a Tutsi lost his cattle, he could be demoted to being a Hutu. Mixed marriages between Hutu and Tutsi were common.

1.2   Influence of colonialism — defining 'race'

At the Berlin Colonial Conference of 1884-1885, the territory of Rwanda was awarded to Germany. As the Germans did not exercise any direct power, but instead attempted to establish colonial rule via local leaders, the *mwami* was urged to strengthen and centralise his authority. Colonial concepts were based on racist views. Drawing on the theory that the Hamites, a people who were related to whites, had brought civilisation to Africa, the Germans chose the Tutsi over the Hutu as the supposed descendants of the Hamites. The German colonisers strengthened the predominant position of the Tutsi.

Hamitic Myth

The Hamitic hypothesis states that 'everything of value ever found in Africa was brought there by the Hamites, allegedly a branch of the Caucasian race.'[4] This 19th Century racist theory was named after Noah's son Ham from the Old Testament. According to this theory, the Hamites came to North Africa during the Stone Age, and spread to the rest of the continent from there. Moving south, the Hamites mixed with the indigenous black peoples of Africa. Racial theory was used to justify European imperialism, in the ideas of French diplomat and politician Arthur de Gobineau (1816-1882). De Gobineau divided mankind into a three-race hierarchy. The Caucasian (Europid) race, according to his theory, was superior. Then came the Mongoloid race, followed by the inferior Negroid or black race.

After the First World War, under the terms of the Treaty of Versailles (1919), Germany was forced to relinquish its colonies. The League of Nations decided to place Rwanda and Burundi under Belgian auspices. Under Belgian rule, the difference in status between the Hutu and Tutsi became socially fixed. A then popular pseudo-scientific, racist method of taking skull and nose measurements was used to determine whether one was a Hutu or a Tutsi. Based on external characteristics, the ethnic origins of all citizens — Hutus, Tutsi and also the Twa — were recorded on their personal identity cards. The entire population was divided into ethnic groups and this was applied to every single aspect of life, including employment agreements and contracts. The Hutu and Tutsi stereotypes would have far-reaching consequences.

The Belgian government only appointed members of the Tutsi elite as officials or mayors. As only the Tutsi had access to schooling, the right to collect taxes and the right to move freely, Tutsi loyalty to the colonial power was guaranteed. The poor masses consisted mainly of Hutus, and Hutu frustrations grew over many years.

2.   Independent Rwanda

From the mid-1950s, a move towards decolonisation took place across nearly all of Asia and Africa. Belgium experienced a particularly tumultuous period in its colonies. The pursuit of independence by many highly-educated Tutsi led to a cooling of relations with the Belgians. The Belgian government was keen to avoid a war of independence and somewhat unexpectedly dropped its policy of favouring the Tutsi. Now, Hutus were admitted to functions and organisations that had until recently been reserved for Tutsi. In 1957, with the approval of the Belgian government, the Party of the Hutu Emancipation Movement, MDR-Parmehutu, was founded.

These developments put a strain on social relations, especially when it became clear that the Hutu were aiming for independence. The Hamitic myth, which had long worked in the Tutsi's favour, now played against them. MDR-Parmehutu leaders proclaimed aggressively that a people that originated in North Africa did not belong in Rwanda. The Tutsi felt threatened. When the *mwami*, the old Tutsi king, died in 1959, the Hutu rose up in revolt against the Tutsi, and the Hutu social revolution was declared. The revolution ended in the first wave of massacres. Thousands of Tutsi were killed during the violence. For the Belgians, it was clear that their colonial powers had come to an end. Elections had to be held. The Belgian government returned its mandate to the United Nations, the successor to the League of Nations.

In the 1960 elections, MDR-Parmehutu emerged as the winner. The result was the immediate overthrow of the monarchy. Tutsi leaders were replaced with Hutu leaders, and tens of thousands of Tutsi fled the country.

In July 1962, Rwanda and Burundi celebrated their independence. The separation of the two countries by the United Nations was followed by rioting. In 1963, Tutsi fighting units attempted to overthrow the regime of the new president, Grégoire Kayibanda of the MDR. But President Kayibanda succeeded in mobilising the existing mainly-Hutu population by playing on fears of renewed Tutsi tyranny. During those days, Kayibanda spoke of the Tutsi as 'cockroaches', vermin that must be exterminated. The Hutu reacted to these words by driving the Tutsi out of their houses and villages. In what became a true exodus, around 300,000 Tutsi fled to Uganda, Tanzania and Burundi. In a repeat of the events at the end of the 1950s, tens of thousands of Rwandan Tutsi were killed, their possessions confiscated by Hutus and by the Rwandan government.

Mwami Mutara III, Tutsi king between 1931 and 1959
Source: Kigali Genocide Memorial Centre

2.1   Rwanda under Habyarimana

Kayibanda's successor, Juvénal Habyarimana, came to power in 1973 by means of a *coup d'état*. Like Kayibanda, Habyarimana's politics were based on ethnic divide and rule. He stuck to the system of ethnic identity cards from the colonial period, now reversed and favouring Hutu over Tutsi. Tutsi participation in education was limited, while mixed marriages were officially outlawed in 1976. Habyarimana also confiscated people's possessions. Some Tutsi were forcibly 'relocated' to heavily forested provinces that had to be cultivated. Ethnically motivated killings also took place in the 1970s. Despite this, the Tutsi minority was relatively safe compared to the situation in the 1950s and 1960s. Habyarimana even favoured a small group of Tutsi, particularly businessmen.

In the 1980s, Rwanda's economy developed into one of the most stable economies in Africa. However, in the mid-1980s, four out of five families still lived in rural areas, and nine out of ten families made a living from agriculture. Figures from 1991 report that the population of Rwanda was around eight million, with 89.9% Hutu and 9.8% Tutsi; the remaining 0.4% was made up of Twa.

3.   The prelude to genocide

At the end of the 1980s, the economy went into a free-fall. Poor harvests led to food shortages. The combination of hunger and the high population density, the growing trade deficit, and increasing corruption and personal enrichment among the elite led to social unrest. Habyarimana was openly criticised, a striking development given that there was no freedom of speech in Rwanda. The French government, which felt partly responsible for African political relations, put pressure on Habyarimana to introduce a multi-party system. From 1991, new radical Hutu parties competed with Habyarimana's MRND for popular support. Habyarimana's politics soon took an extreme course.

By 1990, about one million Rwandan Tutsis were living in exile. The militants among them (including the current president of Rwanda, Paul Kagame) founded an emancipation movement called the Rwandan Patriotic Front (RPF). Their goal was to overthrow Habyarimana and his predominantly Hutu government, and to clear the way for the return of Tutsi exiles from abroad. From October 1990 onwards, RPF militants from Uganda returned to Rwandan territory and blended in with the Tutsi population. The militants called themselves *Inkotanyi*. In 1992, they succeeded in occupying various northern Rwandan provinces, to the horror of both Hutu and Tutsi, who were fearful of reprisal attacks by both the Rwandan army and the RPF. These fears were justified. The Rwandan army struck with a vengeance. Hundreds of Tutsi were killed; the violence went unpunished. Radical Hutu set up their own fighting units to deal with what they called 'unpatriotic elements'. In response, Habyarimana's party created its own paramilitary organisation, the *Interahamwe*.

In 1992, the growing Rwandan army, supported by French 'advisors', was able to halt the advance of the RPF. At this time, Central Africa was plagued by social unrest. The United Nations (UN) turned its attention to the region, and as a result, Habyarimana was forced to join the RPF's leaders at the negotiation table in Arusha, Tanzania, supervised by the UN. Now Habyarimana found himself in a difficult position. While the international community expected him be moderate, his domestic political rhetoric turned extremist. The Tutsi became a scapegoat in Rwandan society.

Arusha Accords

The Arusha Accords are a power-sharing agreement signed in Tanzania in 1993 under international pressure. The aim of these Accords had been to bring about a peaceful end to the situation of crisis and civil war in Rwanda, starting with the formation of a transitional government in which almost all parties involved would participate.

---

4. Ideology, propaganda and hate campaigns

With Habyarimana's approval, a propaganda campaign began, aiming to alienate the Hutu from the Tutsi. The Tutsi, as a scapegoat, were criminalised; a tried-and-tested method that had previously been used by Lenin and Hitler. *Kangura* (Wake Up), an influential Rwandan newspaper, published the 'Hutu Ten Commandments'. These set out rules for Hutu contact with the Tutsi.

Interahamwe, 1993
Source: Kigali Genocide Memorial Centre

Arusha Accords, front left Habyarimana, August 4, 1993
Source: Kigali Genocide Memorial Centre

5. VOICI LES 10 COMMANDE-MENTS.

1. Tout Muhutu doit savoir que Umututsikazi où qu'elle soit, travaille à la solde de son ethnie tutsi. Par conséquent, est traître tout Muhutu:

   — qui épouse une mututsikazi;
   — qui fait d'une Umututsikazi sa concubine;
   — qui fait d'une Umututsikazi sa secrétaire ou sa protégée.

2. Tout Muhutu doit savoir que nos filles Bahutukazi sont plus dignes et plus consciencieuses dans leur rôle de femme, d'épouse et de mère de famille. Ne sont-elles pas jolies, bonnes secrétaires et plus honnêtes!

3. Bahutukazi, soyez vigilantes et ramenez vos maris, vos frères et vos fils à la raison.

4. Tout Muhutu doit savoir que tout Mututsi est malhonnête dans les affaires. Il ne vise que la suprématie de son ethnie.

« RIZABARA UWARIRAYE »

Par conséquent, est traître tout Muhutu:

— qui fait alliance avec les Batutsi dans ses affaires;
— qui investit son argent ou l'argent de l'Etat dans une entreprise d'un Mututsi;
— qui prête ou emprunte de l'argent à un Mututsi;
— qui accorde aux Batutsi des faveurs dans les affaires (l'octroi des licences d'importation, des prêts bancaires, des parcelles de construction, des marchés publics...)

5. Les postes stratégiques tant politiques, administratifs, économiques, militaires et de sécurité doivent être confiés aux Bahutu.

6. Le secteur de l'Enseignement (élèves, étudiants, enseignants) doit être majoritairement Hutu.

7. Les Forces Armées Rwandaises doivent être exclusivement Hutu. L'expérience de la guerre d'octobre 1990 nous l'enseigne. Aucun militaire ne doit épouser une Mututsikazi.

8. Les Bahutu doivent cesser d'avoir pitié des Batutsi.

9. — Les Bahutu, où qu'ils soient, doivent être unis, solidaires et préoccupés du sort de leurs frères Bahutu.
   — Les Bahutu de l'intérieur et de l'extérieur du Rwanda doivent rechercher constamment des amis et des alliés pour la Cause Hutu, à commencer par leurs frères bantous.
   — Ils doivent constamment contrecarrer la propagande tutsi.
   — Les Bahutu doivent être fermes et vigilants contre leur ennemi commun tutsi.

10. La Révolution Sociale de 1959, le Référendum de 1961, et l'Idéologie Hutu, doivent être enseignés à tout Muhutu et à tous les niveaux.
Tout Muhutu doit diffuser largement la présente idéologie.
Est traître tout Muhutu qui persécutera son frère Muhutu pour avoir lu, diffusé et enseigné cette idéologie.

Hutu Ten Commandments, *Kangura*, No 6, 1990
Source: Kigali Genocide Memorial Centre

Hutu Ten Commandments

1. Every Hutu should know that a Tutsi woman, wherever she is, works for the interest of her ethnic Tutsi group. Consequently, we should consider a traitor every Hutu who:

    a. marries a Tutsi woman;

    b. befriends a Tutsi woman;

    c. employs a Tutsi woman as a secretary or concubine.

2. Every Hutu should know that our Hutu daughters are more suitable and dutiful in their roles as women, wives and mothers of the family. Are they not more wonderful, good secretaries and more honest?

3. Hutu women, be vigilant and try to bring your husbands, brothers and sons back to reason.

4. Every Hutu should know that every Tutsi is dishonest in business. Their only aim is supremacy for their ethnic group. As a consequence, every Hutu is a traitor who does the following:

    a. makes a business partnership with a Tutsi;

    b. invests his money or that of the government in a Tutsi enterprise;

    c. lends money to or from a Tutsi;

    d. gives business favours to a Tutsi (obtaining import licences, bank loans, construction sites, public markets etc.).

5. All strategic posts, political, administrative, economic, military and these in the area of security, should be entrusted to Hutus.

6. The majority of the education sector, i.e. school pupils, students, teachers, must be Hutu.

7. The Rwandan armed forces should be exclusively Hutu. The experience of the October War has taught us a lesson. No member of the military shall marry a Tutsi.

8. Hutus should stop having mercy on the Tutsi.

9. The Hutus must, whoever they are, maintain unity and solidarity and be concerned with the fate of their Hutu brothers;

    a. The Hutus in and outside Rwanda must constantly look for friends and allies for the Hutu cause, starting with their own Bantu brothers;

    b. They must constantly counteract Tutsi propaganda;

    c. The Hutus must be firm and vigilant against their common Tutsi enemy.

10. The Social Revolution of 1959, the Referendum of 1961 and Hutu ideology must be taught at every level to every Hutu. Every Hutu must spread this ideology widely. Every Hutu who persecutes his Hutu brother because he has read, spread and taught this ideology is a traitor.

The *Hutu Ten Commandments* aimed to convince the Hutu population that the Tutsi were their archetypal enemies. The propaganda evoked images of war, slavery, oppression, injustice, death and cruelty. Fabricated images of non-existent RPF munitions depots, for example, or shady suspect Tutsi, led Hutus to be fearful and arm themselves in order to protect and defend themselves against the Tutsi enemy.

Despite poor distribution, *Kangura* reached a wide audience. Other newspapers and magazines copied reports that appeared in *Kangura*. Despite the fact that only 66% of Rwandans could read, the propaganda was highly effective: the articles were lavishly illustrated with cartoons that communicated an unmistakably malicious message. Moreover, the Rwandan oral culture meant that the *Hutu Ten Commandments* were passed on to many illiterate people.

Because of the high rate of illiteracy, the radio was the most successful tool for propaganda. In 1991, only 29% of all households owned a radio, but Rwandans who did not have radios listened to broadcasts in local cafes or elsewhere. Until 1992, the country's only station, Radio Rwanda (NNR), mainly broadcast presidential addresses, official governmental announcements, exam results and censored news bulletins. An independent radio station did not exist. When, in 1991, the RPF put its own station, Radio Muhabura, on air, it quickly caught on among Rwandans. In response to this the government founded Radio Télévision Libre des Mille Collines (RTLM). The hugely popular musician Simon Bikindi and all of the RTLM shareholders came from the elite that surrounded Habyarimana. RTLM was soon drawing a large audience. The station's lively music and informal style of presentation encouraged people to tune in. RTLM news bulletins and local news flashes were full of gossip and scandal. Members of the audience were encouraged to phone in, and the callers were put live on air.

The Rwandan intelligentsia was also influenced by the propaganda. Since the educational system was funded by the government, most lecturers saw little room for an independent or critical stance. One of the most influential professors, Léon Mugesera, a hard-line Hutu propagandist made the infamous speech: 'Do not let yourselves be invaded'.

Excerpts of the speech by Léon Mugesera on 22 November 1992

I know you are men [...] who do not let themselves be invaded, who refuse to be scorned. [...] Why do they not arrest these parents who have sent away their children and why do they not exterminate them? Why do they not arrest the people taking them away and why do they not exterminate all of them? Are we really waiting till they come to exterminate us? [...] Rise up [...] really rise up. If you are struck once on one cheek, you should strike back twice.[...] Know that the person whose throat you do not cut now will be the one who will cut yours. [...] If one day someone attacks you with a gun, you will not come to tell us that we [...] did not warn you of it!

The Rwandan newspaper *Kangura*
Photo: Thijs B. Bouwknegt

Mugesera called for self-defence, on the grounds that the enemy was out to destroy *all* Hutus. Quoting from the Bible, Mugesera gave an unusual twist to the principle of 'turn the other cheek'; this became, 'if you are hit on one cheek, hit back twice'. Parts of this speech were broadcast on 22 November 1992, eighteen months before the genocide.

5. United Nations and UNAMIR

While the propaganda machine was operating at full force and Hutu extremists were calling for 'Hutu power', the international community focused its attention on Rwanda. A classified CIA report (January 1993) referred to massive arms purchases — consignments of guns, hand grenades and machetes. The United Nations took the explosive situation to heart and sent observers. The United Nations Assistance Mission for Rwanda, UNAMIR, was installed to help implement a transitional government as agreed in the Arusha Accords. The UNAMIR mandate consisted of peacekeeping, disarmament, supervising the ceasefire and reporting incidents. It was also supposed to assist with the repatriation of refugees and to coordinate humanitarian

Hutu propaganda. 'I am sick, doctor', 'Do you know what makes you sick?', 'The Tutsis, the Tutsis!!!'
Photo: Thijs B Bouwknegt

aid. The mandate explicitly excluded intervention in conflicts.

UNAMIR was headed by the Canadian General Roméo Dallaire. He had 2,548 troops of 26 different nationalities under his command. The former coloniser Belgium also sent troops, even though this was actually not permitted under UN regulations. Belgium provided a battalion of 450 troops and a paramilitary commando. UNAMIR's equipment was inadequate and the mission had a low status.

On the eve of the genocide in Rwanda four different groups were competing for power in the political and social arena. Firstly the moderate Hutus led by Prime Minister Uwilingiymana and supported by UNAMIR. Then there were Hutu extremists, supported by the army, the Interahamwe and other youth militias, and also by the media (such as Kangura, RTLM, NNR). Thirdly there was the RPF, and lastly UNAMIR. Uwilingiymana's transitional government, the small moderate Hutu parties and UNAMIR followed the same lines. The Hutu extremists and the RPF were diametrically opposed. As the Hutu extremists called for 'Hutu power', lists of the names of the president's political opponents were ready and waiting in Kigali. Habyarimana wanted to maintain his power at any cost.

6. Genocide

On the evening of Wednesday 6 April 1994, the presidential aeroplane approached the airport of Kigali. On board were the Rwandan president Juvenal Habyarimana, Chief-of-Staff of the Rwandan army General Deogratias Nsabimana, President Cyprien Ntayamira of Burundi and other Rwandan political and military authorities. They had been at a meeting of heads of state from the region at which Habyarimana had finally agreed to implement the Arusha Accords. While the French air crew started on the long descent, two missiles were fired from the ground close to the airport. The first missile hit a wing, the second the aircraft's tail. According to eyewitnesses the plane caught fire immediately and after an enormous explosion landed in the grounds of

Fragment ICTR Cartoonbook p. 15
Source: ICTR

the nearby President's palace. No one in the plane survived the crash.

Immediately after Habyarimana's death UNAMIR General Roméo Dallaire went to the Rwandan Army's headquarters, where he met Colonel Théoneste Bagosora, a Hutu hardliner. Dallaire stated that Habyarimana's death meant that Prime Minister Agathe Uwilingiyimana had automatically become the legal head of state.

6.1 The killing starts in Kigali

In the hours following Habyarimana's assassination, Rwandan military units moved through Kigali. Within twelve hours many Tutsi elite and all moderate Hutus in influential positions in Kigali were murdered. Among the first victims were Prime Minister Agathe Uwilingiyimana and her husband, the Minister of Agriculture, and the Minister of Labour. The fifteen UN soldiers guarding the Prime Minister were imprisoned. Within a few hours the streets of Kigali had been taken over by armed Hutus who put up road blocks to prevent anyone from escaping the city. The streets of Kigali were systematically ransacked, and all suspect Tutsi or moderate Hutu were killed.

The RTLM radio station started to name Tutsi and moderate Hutu with their addresses and number plates during their broadcasts. If your name was mentioned on the radio, everyone immediately understood that you were being looked for and would be killed by the Interahamwe. Right from the beginning of the genocide, the RTLM supported the Interahamwe by passing on information during broadcasts about the direction in which victims were trying to escape. After a few days thousands of decomposing corpses were piled high in the streets of Kigali.

6.2 Genocide in rural areas

About a week after the outbreak of mass violence in the capital, massacres started to take place in rural areas. This illustrates how carefully things were planned in advance. Orders were passed down from above through the administrative machinery. Prefects informed mayors and subprefects, who in turn explained to their closest staff members how the commands were to be passed on to the actual murderers. In most cases school and hospital directors, local councillors and businessmen were involved in the murder plans. Because of their authority and influence they were instrumental in inciting ordinary people to carry out the killing.

'They told where to go to kill and which route to take down into the marshlands. ...Then we separated into small groups of acquaintances or friends. It was a collusion that didn't cause any problems. Except on busy days, when *Interahamwes* with motor vehicles came from the surrounding regions as back-up for a big operation. Those men were so fired up they made it hard for us to work. The councillor told us all we were expected to do was kill Tutsi. We understood very well that fixed plans had been made. [...] So the only questions asked were about organisational details, such as how, when and also where we were supposed to start, because we were not used to operations like this, and the Tutsi had escaped in all

Victims, Kigali Genocide Memorial Centre
Photo: Thijs B. Bouwknegt

directions. Someone even asked if there were preferences. The councillor replied sternly: "The question is not where you should start, the only right way is close by, in the bush, and right now, without asking any questions.[...]"'[5]

Genocidaire

Whereas in Kigali the murderers had been well-equipped government troops and militiamen with automatic rifles and hand grenades, in rural areas simple farmers murdered with machetes, knives, spears, wooden clubs studded with nails, and screwdrivers. Because initially the murderers were not very skilled or experienced, these primitive methods of massacre were bloodier than in the capital.

'At first we were too fired up to think. Later it had become too much of a habit. In the state we were in it meant nothing to us that we were chopping off all our neighbours' heads. It had become a matter of course. By then they were no longer our good neighbours from way back who used to pass us the bottle at the pub, because they were no longer allowed to go there. They had become people who had to be cleared away, so to speak. They were no longer what they had been, and neither were we. We didn't feel bothered by them or by the past, because we didn't feel bothered by anything.[...] We had to leave any friendly feelings behind at the edge of the swamp until the signal had been given that our work was finished. Good manners were not permitted in the swamp either. No exceptions were possible in the swamp. We were so ferocious and hardened that we just kept killing and because of that forgot about any doubts.[...] Some men started on the hunt in good spirits and finished in good spirits. And other men were never keen at all and killed because they were obliged to.[...] The more you killed, the more you were urged on by greed to continue.[...] A man can get used to killing if he constantly kills. He can even become a wild beast and not pay any attention to it. Some men started to threaten each other when there were no more Tutsi to use their machetes on. You could see from their faces that they felt the need to kill.'[6]

Genocidaire

The RTLM played a different role in spreading the genocide in rural areas. In Kigali the *Interahamwe* and *Impuzamugambi* were informed through RTLM radio about which Tutsi were trying to escape by pretending to be Hutu, but in the countryside hills people knew each other's ethnicity. *Genocidaires* knew their victims, they lived near and with each other, helped each other, had listened to the radio together in cafes. They were neighbours, knew each other's children and grandchildren, or had been to school together.

For days and weeks in succession victims sought shelter in the marshes, steeped in mud, hiding behind eucalyptus trees and banana leaves. After the *genocidaires* had returned home the Tutsi came out of their hiding places to count the dead. In the evening they shared their food and went to look for water for yet another day of killing. Some died of exhaustion, some surrendered to the murderers to be killed so as to be delivered from their misery.

'The morning after the President's plane was shot down, I was in my uncle's house with five cousins. The *Interahamwe* came, saying they were going to rape the girls. Uncle Gashugi pleaded with them not to do it, but they cut him down with a machete. I ran out of the back door with the others. All the other girls were killed before they reached the gate. I'm the only one of the household who survived. I went from house to house, like a hunted animal. Sometimes I hid in the drains with the corpses, pretending to be dead myself.'[7]

Béatha Uwazaninka, survivor Rwandan genocide

It was easier to hide in the countryside than it was in Kigali. Escaping the city was virtually impossible because of the many roadblocks. In the country the victims were relatively safe at night. Sometimes young women survived after being sexually abused by Hutu, but often rape was followed by murder.

Between 6 April and the end of June 1994, in just 100 days, approximately three quarters of the total Tutsi population of Rwanda was killed. Estimates of the number of victims vary between 507,000 (Human Rights Watch's historian and ICTR expert witness Alison Des Forges) and 1.2 million (Rwandan government). The latter figure includes the ongoing killings in the refugee camps in Congo.

In the subsequent months, large-scale crimes were again committed, but now Hutus were the victims and most of the perpetrators were RPF fighting units. In July 1994 more than two million Hutus took flight and hundreds of thousands of Tutsi came to Rwanda from neighbouring countries.

7. Aftermath

On 8 November 1994 the UN Security Council decided to set up a tribunal to prosecute persons responsible for genocide and other serious violations of international humanitarian law committed in Rwanda and abroad between 1 January and 31 December 1994. Rwanda, a temporary council member in 1994, was the only country to vote against the tribunal. The International Criminal Tribunal for Rwanda (ICTR) was established in Arusha, Tanzania, in the same building where the Arusha Accords were signed. It has to complete its work by 2013.

Gacaca

After the genocide, more than 100,000 Hutu were imprisoned on suspicion of having participated in the 1994 genocide. It would have taken decades to bring each alleged perpetrator to justice individually. Also, these men were needed to rebuild the country. National means of coming to terms with the atrocities came from the traditional community-based gacaca courts. The gacaca courts aimed to reveal the truth about what has happened, to speed up the genocide trials, to eradicate the culture of impunity and to reconcile the Rwandans and reinforce their unity. Some 12,000 gacaca courts dealt with over a million cases.

'There are still people with such bestial hearts; people who killed. You can tell they would do it again. Reconciliation is not the problem. The problem is that those who killed, ate our cattle and took our things, run away from us. I don't know how we can forgive when there hasn't been any communication between us. There are lots of people like that who look at you and wish you were dead.'[8]

Emmanuel Mugenzira, survivor Rwandan genocide

114

Gacaca Hearing (above) and Court (below)
Photo: Thijs B. Bouwknegt

Gacaca Judges
Photo: Thijs B. Bouwknegt

The current Rwandan president Paul Kagame strongly denies the charge that the crimes of the RPF against the Hutus were genocidal in nature. The academic and political discussion is still in full swing.

7.1 International Responses, Intervention and prevention

The international community had been painfully unable to intervene or prevent the atrocities. It was unable to draw the right conclusions on time. In the first days of April 1994, the term 'ethnic cleansing' was used instead of genocide. UN General Roméo Dallaire, probably the best-known witness ('bystander') to the genocide, said that although he was initially appalled by the murders, he had the impression that the Rwandan army and the *Interahamwe* were attacking political enemies of Habyarimana. It was only in the course of several days that it began to dawn on him that crimes against humanity were being committed and that *all* Tutsi were being targeted. He only realised this when he actually saw *Interahamwe* pulling people with Tutsi ID cards out of their cars at roadblocks and murdering them on the spot.

> 'I just needed a slap in the face to say, "This is genocide, not just ethnic cleansing". [...] I was self-conscious about saying the killings were "genocidal" because genocide was the equivalent of the Holocaust or the Killing Fields of Cambodia — I mean millions of people. [...] "Ethnic cleansing" seemed to involve thousands of people. Genocide was the highest scale of crimes against humanity imaginable. It was so far up there, so far off the charts, that it was not easy to recognise that we could be in such a situation.'
> General Roméo Dallaire

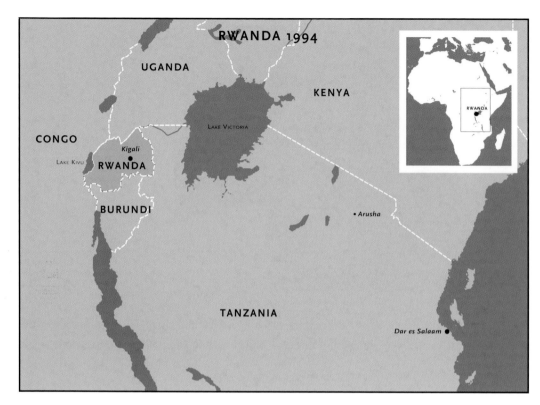

Théoneste Bagosora at the ICTR
Source: Kigali Genocide Memorial
Centre

Théoneste Bagosora (b. 1941)
Military officer, is allegedly the mastermind of the genocide. He was responsible for establishing the Interahamwe and distributing arms and machetes throughout Rwanda. Bagosora was convicted on the counts of genocide, crimes against humanity and war crimes.

Roméo Dallaire (b. 1946)
Force Commander of UNAMIR, the ill-fated United Nations peacekeeping force for Rwanda between 1993 and 1994.

Juvénal Habyarimana (1937-1994)
President of Rwanda from 1973 to 1994. His assassination is generally believed to have sparked the Rwandan genocide.

Paul Kagame (b. 1957)
Leader of the Rwandan Patriotic Front (RPF), whose victory over the incumbent government in July 1994 effectively ended the Rwandan genocide. Current president of Rwanda.

Léon Mugesera (b. 1952)
Mugesera was a member of the MRND party and a professor of political science. He was a Hutu-propagandist, infamous for his inflammatory anti-Tutsi speech. He fled to Canada, where he still resides.

General Roméo Dallaire
Source: Kigali Genocide Memorial
Centre

Agathe Uwilingiyimana (1953-1994)
Prime Minister of Rwanda from 18 July 1993 until her death on 7 April 1994. She was assassinated during the opening stages of the Rwandan Genocide.

Glossary

CDR	Hutu Coalition for the Defence of the Republic.
ICTR	International Criminal Tribunal for Rwanda.
Interahamwe	Hutu militias linked to the MRND.
Impuzamugamabi	Hutu militia linked to the extremist CDR.
Inkotanyi	RPF militants from Uganda returned on Rwandan territory and blended in with the Tutsi population.
Kangura	Influential Rwandan newspaper. Translated: Wake Up.
Machete	A cleaver, an agricultural tool, used as a weapon during the Rwandan genocide.
MDR-Parmehutu	Party of the Hutu Emancipation Movement.
MRND	Habyarimana's National Revolutionary Movement for Development.
Mwami	The king, who came from the Tutsi community.
NNR	Until 1992, the country's only radio station, Radio Rwanda.
RPF	Rwandan Patriotic Front.
RTLM	Radio Télévision Libre des Mille Collines. Supported the Interahamwe, spreading information about the ongoing genocide.
UNAMIR	United Nations Assistance Mission for Rwanda.

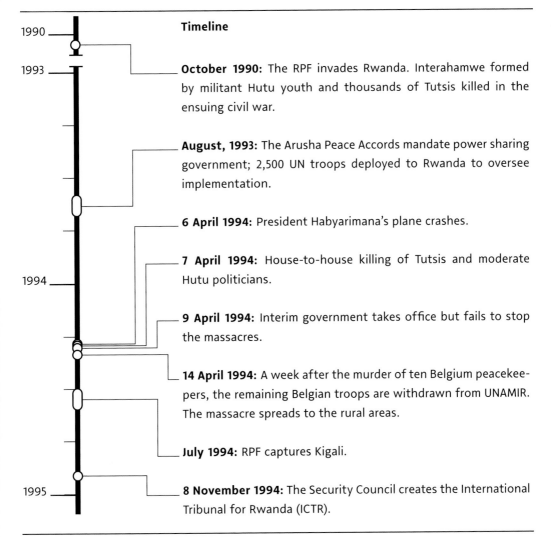

	Timeline
1990	
1993	**October 1990:** The RPF invades Rwanda. Interahamwe formed by militant Hutu youth and thousands of Tutsis killed in the ensuing civil war.
	August, 1993: The Arusha Peace Accords mandate power sharing government; 2,500 UN troops deployed to Rwanda to oversee implementation.
	6 April 1994: President Habyarimana's plane crashes.
1994	**7 April 1994:** House-to-house killing of Tutsis and moderate Hutu politicians.
	9 April 1994: Interim government takes office but fails to stop the massacres.
	14 April 1994: A week after the murder of ten Belgium peacekeepers, the remaining Belgian troops are withdrawn from UNAMIR. The massacre spreads to the rural areas.
	July 1994: RPF captures Kigali.
1995	**8 November 1994:** The Security Council creates the International Tribunal for Rwanda (ICTR).

Notes

1 Hatzfield, J. (2006). *Machete Season: The killers in Rwanda speak*. London. In addition, Hatzfeld has also written about Rwandan survivors: *Into the quick of life. The Rwandan Genocide: the survivors speak*, London 2005.

2 Source: http://www.kigalimemorialcentre.org/old/survivors/valentine.html.

3 The Hutu and Tutsi abbreviations came into use mostly after the 1994 genocide.

4 Sander, E.R. (1969). 'The Hamitic Hypothesis: its origin in time perspective'. In: *Journal of African History*, x, 4, 521-532: 521.

5 Hatzfield, idem, pp. 16-27

6 Idem, pp. 57-62

7 A longer version of this account is published by the Aegis Trust in '*A Time to Remember: Rwanda, ten years after the genocide*'

8 Idem.

Surivivors of the attack on Srebrenica arrive
at a United Nations camp.
Photo: Ron Haviv

Crisis and Genocide in Yugoslavia, 1985-1995

Ton Zwaan

'Dear Mimmy,
More journalists, reporters and cameramen. They write, take photographs, film, and it all goes
to France, Italy, Canada, Japan, Spain, America. But you and I, Mimmy, we stay where we are,
we stay and we wait, and, of course, keep each other company. Some people compare me with
Anne Frank. That frightens me, Mimmy, I don't want to suffer her fate.'[1]
Zlata, 12 years old

This comparison with Anne Frank, albeit hardly justified, made Zlata instantly famous. While Sarajevo was still under siege she was visited by journalists and reporters and parts of her diary were published. Due to her success as a writer, Zlata and her family were 'rescued' by her publisher and brought to safety in Paris.

Yugoslavia signs Genocide Convention, 1948.
Source: United Nations

Introduction

The war in Yugoslavia took place before the eyes of the world, being widely broadcasted. But instead of intervening, for the most part the world followed the atrocities on television. The bewildering complexity of the civil war did not help. People witnessed Serbs fighting Muslim Bosnians and Croats, Croats fighting Serbs and Muslim Bosnians, Muslim Bosnians fighting Croats and Serbs, and this all took place in what had been, at least superficially, considered the rather peaceful and ethnically mixed socialist federal state of Yugoslavia.

1. Historical Background

To understand the conflict, it is important to take a look at the history of Yugoslavia. The six republics which formed the federal state — Slovenia, Croatia, Bosnia and Herzegovina, Serbia, Montenegro, and Macedonia — shared a complicated and often violent past. The development of a power vacuum after 1980, serious political and economic problems including the issue of multiple nationalities, the decline of communism in neighbouring countries and in the country itself, followed by a turn to extreme nationalism, polarisation and the disintegration of the monopoly of violence, all contributed to the end of Yugoslavia.

Yugoslavia, a country roughly seven times the size of the Netherlands, about half the size of France, and formerly inhabited by approximately 24 million people, no longer exists. After an in many ways difficult, tragic and turbulent development of less than 75 years as a relatively autonomous state-society, it disintegrated in only a few years. The decade between 1985 — when the threatening disintegration became more and more apparent — and 1995 — when the Dayton Agreement was signed on 21 November, thus ending the three and a half years of fighting in Bosnia and Herzegovina — was of decisive importance for the disintegration of the federal state.

What became Yugoslavia after the First World War (1914-1918) was for many centuries a pre-eminent example of a disputed frontier territory. In addition to the original ethnic-cultural variety in the region, Islam and Christianity encountered each other here, and the dividing line between western (Roman-Catholic) and eastern (Orthodox) Christianity cut clear across the country between the two largest sections of the population, the Croats and the Serbs. In this region 'Europe' gradually changed into 'the Orient', and the Austro-Hungarian and Ottoman Empires fought frequently and extensively. Between the late 14th and the late 15th century the Ottoman Empire conquered a large part of the Balkans — including Macedonia, Serbia, parts of Montenegro, and Bosnia and Herzegovina, but not Croatia and Slovenia. These latter became part of the Austro-Hungarian Empire.

The Habsburg and Ottoman Empires both recruited soldiers and militias from the local peasant population. In the battles of the 19th century, when the Ottoman Empire was driven back from the Balkans, culminating in the wars of 1912 and 1913, excessive violence was common. This affected armies on all sides as well as the civilian population.

Often lacking the protection of a reliable state authority, the peasant population had to rely on themselves for the protection of their lives, goods and honour. Blood feuds, vendettas, and banditry were widespread. For generations, large parts of the mostly rural population lived under harsh and violent conditions. A glance through history shows that the region experienced no significant period of peace in at least 150 years. A 'culture of violence' was manifested in aggressively masculine ideals, combining warrior notions with a predilection for weapons and the skill to use them. The population was willing and able to use force, and was easily caught up in revenge and counter revenge. For many, this resulted in a relatively limited sensitivity to violence.

1.2   The Kingdom of Serbs, Croats and Slovenes

At the end of the First World War, the new state of Yugoslavia — under the name of the Kingdom of Serbs, Croats, and Slovenes — consisted of territories and population groups with diverse ethno-cultural and political traditions. Considerable parts of the newly formed kingdom had been part of the two disintegrating empires, and had been at war between 1914 and 1918. Several contemporary observers therefore questioned the viability of the new Kingdom of Serbs, Croats, and Slovenes. The former kingdom of Serbia acquired a dominant position in the new state. The Serbian elite became the elite of the new kingdom; its capital, Belgrade, became the capital of the kingdom; and Serbian troops, only marginally assisted by Croatian and Slovene soldiers, occupied the whole territory of the new Yugoslav kingdom in 1918 and 1919.

As a result, considerable parts of the non-Serbian population, especially in Slovenia and Croatia, felt they had been annexed by Serbia. Callous Serbian policies contributed to growing resentment among Croats and Slovenes, who often considered themselves culturally superior to the Serbs. Serbs, in their turn, fought heroically during the war and had suffered huge losses. These sacrifices were not fully appreciated by the Croats and Slovenes, which was considered 'ungrateful' by the Serbs and led to further tensions.

The new state quickly developed from a weak democracy into an authoritarian monarchist-militaristic dictatorship. The majority of the population had very little opportunity to exert any notable influence on the structure of rule. The political autonomy of the state in the interwar decades was extensive.[2] This meant that the state elites had considerable power of decision and latitude, and no accountability to the population. The ruling apparatus did not tolerate political opposition. This led to violent political assaults and terrorist attacks as well as a few peasant uprisings. Thousands were imprisoned for political reasons. Another important feature of this state formation was a severely limited identification of the population with the new state. Although Yugoslav nationalism and patriotism were imposed by the regime, the different ethnic groups continued to be strongly divided.

1.3   Second World War

The violent German invasion in April 1941 intensified the bitter internal conflict and fighting. It has been estimated that a total of around one million people perished, possibly 300,000 of them in Bosnia and Herzegovina. Individual and collective memories of that time played an important role in the crisis of the 1990s.

During the Second World War, armed groups claiming allegiance to various ideologies and ethnic factions fought both against each other and against the Nazi occupiers. Croatian fascists (Ustaše) launched genocidal campaigns against Serbs and Jews and were notorious for killing Serbs, Jews, Gypsies, Communists, and political opponents. The nationalist and royalist Serb Chetniks were also responsible for many mass killings. The Communist-led Partisans fought against both groups and were victorious (with allied support) at the war's end. The Partisans then unleashed genocidal violence against both Ustaše, Chetniks, and ethnic Germans and killed tens of thousands of perceived political opponents in the first years after the war. From 1945 on, the Partisan leader, Josip Broz Tito, ruled the country as a one-party socialist state.[3]

1.4   Marshall Tito

The federal and communist 'people's republic' in fact continued much of the pre-war state structure. Yugoslavia did not become a pluralistic democracy, nor a constitutional state, but a communist-militaristic dictatorship in which the party — later called the Communist League — dealt with opponents, whether real or imagined, thoroughly and violently.

The new communist state built an extensive repressive apparatus with an all-powerful secret service — modelled on the Soviet NKVD — a large police force, and a massive army. The supremacy of the party and the monopoly of coercive force of the party-state were maintained by these institutions. The old royal court was replaced by a more centralised court in which one

man — Tito — ruled supreme. The now communist political-bureaucratic elites obtained great
decisive power. Very little opposition was allowed, and the population's political influence was extremely limited.

2. Nationalism and increasing polarisation

2.1 Issue of the nationalities

Tito and the other central and republican leaders in the new Yugoslav federation were very much aware of the precarious 'nationalities issue'. Initially, 'collaborators', 'fascists', 'royalists', 'nationalists' and 'counter-revolutionaries' were persecuted. On the one hand supposedly 'national' sensitivities of the most important ethnic categories among the population were taken into account. Governmental, administrative and cultural organisations had to be made up of different ethnic groups. The concept of 'dual sovereignty' was assigned to the different republics as well as to the individual 'nations'. Paradoxically, political or cultural manifestations of group nationalism, other than those officially permitted (traditional costumes, music, songs, etcetera), were strictly taboo, and any politically nationalist activity was out of the question. Officially, the slogan was 'Unity and Brotherhood'; in reality, the situation was one of 'divide and rule'.

The overwhelming majority still tended to define themselves as 'Slovene', 'Serb', 'Croat', or 'Muslim'. It can be concluded that the process of nation formation still remained quite fragile and the population's identification with the state and the identification of the ethnic-national groups with each other remained limited. The issue of nationality never entered the public debate, due to the lack of political, cultural, and intellectual freedom, and society never came to terms with the collective and individual traumas from its recent war history. At the end of the 1980s the repression would return with a vengeance.

After the death of Marshall Tito, 'president for life' of Yugoslavia, who passed away in 1980 at the age of 87 without having appointed a successor, the country was faced with a number of serious problems: the power vacuum after the death of Tito, the degree of centralisation, the nationalities question, and serious economic issues. Managing these four problems, which were interrelated in several ways, was a formidable and difficult task for the Yugoslav leadership. It became even more difficult when two additional problems emerged during the 1980s. The first of these was internal: the rising demands of various groups and parties for more political and economic autonomy; the second was external: the fast changes in international relations, mainly as a consequence of the crumbling of communism in Europe and the end of the Cold War.

2.2 Signs of crisis

One of the first signs of crisis for Yugoslavia in the era after 1980 was a rising demand for Albanian autonomy in the southern province of Kosovo. In effect, Kosovo was already governed by a largely Albanian communist elite — Albanians made up nearly 80% of the population of the province — but now they demanded independence from Serbia and a status equal to that of the six republics. Many Serbs, however, regarded Kosovo as an integral and unalienable part of Serbia.

In the spring of 1981, the Albanian autonomy movement, supported by large groups of the Albanian population in the province, was violently repressed by the police and the federal army of the nationalist Serbian leadership. By 1989, Kosovan autonomy had been completely abolished. This showed that the dominant Yugoslav and Serbian leadership lacked the ability, courage and imagination to handle the rising demands for more freedom in the early eighties in any other way than through fierce repression.

In reaction to this movement, Serbian ethnic-nationalist activism arose among the small Serbian and Montenegrin minority in Kosovo. Propaganda depicted Albanians as primitive barbarians who bred too many children in an effort to outnumber other races. They were accused of wanting to kill hard-working Serbian and Montenegrin peasants, take away their land, and rape their women. Albanians supposedly wished for Kosovo's secession from Serbia and unification with Albania. Although there were almost no factual grounds for these statements, they fed existing feelings of anxiety and threat among local Serbs.

This mechanism of polarisation would often repeat itself in the next decades in Yugoslavia. When faced with circumstances of rising instability and insecurity, groups of people start to perceive other groups as potentially threatening and feel they might become victims. This fear of enemies becomes mind-narrowing and a self-fulfilling prophecy that can only be fought with violence.

3. Serbian Memorandum

In 1986, a group of Serb intellectuals and writers from the Serbian Academy of Arts and Sciences in Belgrade drew up a document, the so-called Serbian Memorandum. This Memorandum presented a radical ethnic-nationalist view of Serbia's position in Yugoslavia. Under Tito's rule, according to the authors, Serbia had always been treated unjustly. The Serbs felt they made the largest military contributions during the World Wars, and suffered more than others. But they had won the war and lost the peace: Serbia was considered the victim of ongoing Slovenian and Croatian political and economic discrimination within the federation. Serbs outside central Serbia, especially in Croatia and Kosovo, were exceptionally poor. These Serbs were considered to be in immediate danger and under the threat of total genocide. Resolution of the Serbian 'national question' had to be given instant and absolute political priority, or the consequences would be incalculable.

According to the Memorandum, the ideal of an independent Greater Serbia was still as valid as ever. It was considered that the only means of securing 'the survival and development' of the Serbs and achieving the 'territorial unity of the Serbian people was by uniting all Serbs in one Serbian national state'. 'Establishing the full national integrity of the Serbian people, irrespective of which republic or province it inhabits, is the Serbian people's historical and democratic right.' It was a direct attack on the foundations of the Yugoslav state-society and the idea of 'Yugoslavism'.

Excerpt from the Memorandum:

'The attitude taken by those in power and the authorities in Kosovo towards the violence directed at the Serbian people is particularly significant. The hushing up or glossing over of these crimes, the practice of suppressing the whole truth, and dilatory tactics in enquiries and prosecution all encourage large and small acts of terror, and at the same time a false, "sanitised" picture of conditions in Kosovo is created. Moreover, there is a persistent tendency to find a political excuse for the violence perpetrated against Serbs in the alleged existence of hatred on both sides, intolerance, and vindictiveness, while of late more and more is being heard of the imaginary activities of an "external" enemy from outside the Province, viz., Serbian nationalism emanating from "Belgrade".'

'Serbia's economic subordination cannot be fully understood without mention of its politically inferior status, from which all other relationships flowed. As far as the Communist Party of Yugoslavia (CPY) was concerned, the economic hegemony of the Serbian nation between the two world wars was beyond dispute, regardless of the fact that Serbia's rate of industrialisation was lower than the Yugoslav average. This ideological platform gave rise to opinions and behaviour which were to have a crucial influence on subsequent political events and inter-communal relations.'

'The Serbian Academy of Sciences and Arts once again expresses its willingness to do everything it can, to the best of its abilities, to assist efforts to deal with these crucial tasks and the historical duties incumbent upon our generation.'

The Serbian Memorandum appealed to considerable numbers of Serbs from all layers in society, within as well as outside the party. Serbian party leader Slobodan Milošević was well aware of this and largely adopted the ideological diagnosis of the Memorandum, making it his own programme. He was subsequently able to bring down other communist leaders in Serbia, strengthen his own power base and that of his lieutenants and allies, and initiate a process of ethnic-nationalist reorientation, unitarism and renewed centralisation in Serbia. Few means were shunned. His tactics included political intrigue within the party and purges, press campaigns, television manipulation, and stage-managed mass demonstrations, for which 'the masses' were transported across Serbia on buses and were brought into action for manifestations in other republics by the same means.

> **Kosovo Polje, April 1987**
>
> **Slobodan Milošević, the communist leader who up until that time had not been very out-spoken in the nationalist debate, travelled to Kosovo Polje, to the historic grounds of the Battle of Kosovo. Here he addressed the Serbian crowds in an orchestrated demonstration: 'Comrades, comrades!' Then someone in the audience shouted at him 'The Albanians got in among us. We were beaten up. Please! They're beating us up!' Milošević then spoke ominous words that would prove to be a turning point in his career as a Serbian leader: 'No one should dare to beat you again!'**
>
> **Later he told his audience: 'This is your land, your fields, your gardens, your memories are here. Surely you will not leave your land because it is difficult here and you are oppressed... You should also stay here because of your ancestors and because of your descendants. Otherwise you would disgrace your ancestors, and disappoint your descendants. I do not propose, comrades, that in staying you should suffer and tolerate a situation in which you are not satisfied. On the contrary you should change it.'[4]**

Instead of carefully curtailing ethnic nationalism, it had now been openly proclaimed a political priority. Communist ideology was replaced by a radical Serb nationalist ideology. The masses were now mobilised in a pseudo-democratic, populist way. This process of polarisation further destabilised the Yugoslav federal state. And although there was some moderate and liberal opposition in Serbia against the increasingly nationalist course, it proved itself too weak to stem the swelling nationalistic tide.

Serbian nationalism provoked the neighbouring republics. Shortly after the Serbian Memorandum was published, the 'Contributions to the Slovene National Programme' appeared in Slovenia. The document called for closing the Slovene ranks, criticised communism, denounced the large economic and financial contribution of Slovenia to the federation, and suggested that perhaps Slovenia would do better to withdraw from Yugoslavia. Partly due to heavy pressure from Belgrade and the national army JNA (*Jugoslovenska Narodna Armija*), the Slovene communist leadership initially rejected these ideas publicly, but growing Serb nationalism led to a rapprochement between the communist establishment and the dissident elite in Slovenia. In rapid succession the leadership decided upon a multi-party system, free elections, a thorough and largely covert preparation for national independence, the proclamation of sovereignty in September 1989 and, after many political entanglements that led to a further radicalisation of points of view, independence in June 1991.

Croatia also responded to the Serbian nationalist mobilisation. A previous revival of Croatian nationalism within the party and in cultural organisations had been forcibly repressed around 1970. Part of the political and intellectual party officials had been purged, some had fled, others, including the former partisan leader, JNA general and military historian Franjo Tuđman, had been imprisoned. Croatia bordered on Serbia and there was a sizeable Serbian minority of more

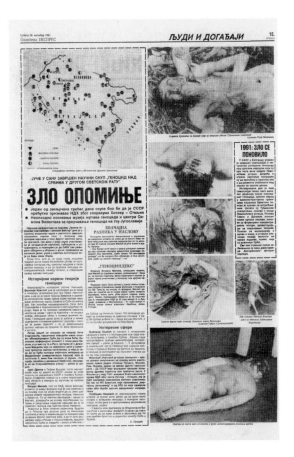

Articles in Serbian press: 'Scholarly conference "Genocide of Serbs in the Second World War" completed yesterday in Serbian Academy of Arts and Sciences: The Evil is Warning'. '1991: The Evil is repeating, with photos of "Serbian victims"'
Source: *Politika Ekspres*, 26 October 1991, p. 15

than half a million people that was well represented in the government, the administration, and the republican police force. However, as Serb nationalism radicalised, the Croatian elite became increasingly worried. This radicalisation was accompanied by harsh campaigns in the Serbian mass media against Muslims, Croats, and against the spectre of the fascist Ustaša regime of the 1940s. In 1989 the nationalist-Croatian Democratic Union, HDZ (*Hrvatska Demokratska Zajednica*), was founded, headed by Franjo Tuđman. Under his populist leadership, ethnic nationalism was no longer restrained, and the Croatian population was politically mobilised, just like in Serbia.

The rise of 'Croatian fascism'

After a multi-party system and elections were decided upon in late 1989, the HDZ started a Croatian nationalist campaign. This campaign purposefully linked up with old Croatian symbols, dreams of a Greater Croatia, and the past of the Ustaša movement, both before and during the Second World War. The campaign focused on the potential Serb threat and the imagined barbaric nature of the Serbs. During mass rallies Tuđman permitted himself remarks like: 'Thank God, my wife isn't Jewish or Serbian', and: 'Bosnia and Herzegovina is a national state of the Croat nation', which were warmly applauded. Furthermore, communities of Croatian emigrants abroad, partly formed of Croats who had taken flight in 1945 and partly Croats that had fled around 1970, were mobilised.

The polarisation process within Yugoslavia was propelled forward. In April 1990 the HDZ won the elections by a narrow margin and in May Tudman became president of Croatia. The declaration of independence followed in June 1991.

4. From political polarisation to mass violence

Yugoslavia was neither a democracy nor a constitutional state. The forces of the monopoly of violence — the police, the army, and various secret services — were neutral institutions only to a limited degree. Nevertheless, individual and collective violence in daily life was relatively rare.

The Yugoslav People's Army JNA contained around 70,000 officers, approximately 70% of whom were Serbs and Montenegrins. The great majority of the officers corps considered the JNA predominantly as the national guardian of the Yugoslav federation and of party communism. The national strategic doctrine anticipated possible hostile attacks, and as Bosnia-Herzegovina formed the central part of the country, large military installations and supplies were concentrated there.

Parallel to the national army, a semi-military organisation was set up, the so-called Territorial Defence Forces TO (*Teritorijalna Odbrana*). These forces were organised per republic and each consisted of several tens of thousands of workers, peasants, and civilians. Trained and equipped, they could mobilise quickly in the event of enemy attack and could then operate as guerrilla troops. The TO had its own command structure and its own, mostly light, arms and supplies. The TO meant that many Yugoslav males had military training and experience. Considerable stocks of weapons and ammunition were available everywhere, and people could easily gain access to these stocks.

The emergence of paramilitary armed groups, militias or gangs, and of local warlords, operating either in close collaboration with the regular forces of the JNA, the Croatian and later the Bosnian-Serb army, or more independently, played an important role in the turn towards violence. Once the chain of decisions of the various political elites in Belgrade, Zagreb, and later also Sarajevo, had opened the way to civil war and war, first in Slovenia, then Croatia and subsequently in Bosnia, the paramilitary groups became active. They were responsible for many of the most extreme atrocities against defenceless citizens committed in Yugoslavia in the first half of the 1990s.

Serb paramilitaries burn the Croatian flag as they take over a town, Autumn 1991.
Photo: Ron Haviv

A member of the Tigers, a Serbian paramilitary group, kicks the dying bodies of the first Muslims to be killed in the war in Bosnia, Spring 1992.
Photo: Ron Haviv

4.1 Conflict and war in Bosnia-Herzegovina

'You want to take Bosnia and Herzegovina down the same highway to hell and suffering that Slovenia and Croatia are travelling. Do not think that you will not lead Bosnia and Herzegovina into hell, and do not think that you will not perhaps lead the Muslim people into annihilation, because the Muslims cannot defend themselves if there is war — How will you prevent everyone from being killed in Bosnia and Herzegovina?'

Radovan Karadžić, October 1991

In March/April 1992, war spread to Bosnia and Herzegovina, the central republic of Yugoslavia, when the JNA and Serbian forces attacked several cities close to the border with Serbia in the north of the republic. In early March 1992 Bosnia and Herzegovina was proclaimed an independent state by the government under Bosnian president Izetbegovic. Soon after this fighting broke out in and around Sarajevo, the capital of the republic turned state. This war lasted for three and a half years, until November 1995.

The course of the war reflected the complicated ethnic and ideological composition of the population of former Yugoslavia, especially in Bosnia and Herzegovina. At least ten armed factions, sometimes in shifting alliances, participated in the fighting. These were mostly Serbian, Croatian, and Muslim Bosnian.

Many people were killed in the war. Some civilian casualties were a result of the fighting, but most were due to widespread so-called ethnic cleansing, which in many cases was nothing more or less than genocidal practices. Ethnic cleansing resulted in large streams of refugees and caused enormous material damage.

Ethnic cleansing

This term is euphemistically used by perpetrators to hide their real intentions and practices. It is well to remember that such practices imply sustained, hostile and violent activities by an organised actor against a largely defenceless population group, whose members are targeted simply because they are perceived to belong to the group. However, it is not easy to attain more precision on these points — a problem frequently encountered in cases of war and civil war, massacres and genocide.

---

5. Victims

A United Nations Commission estimated that by late 1994 around 200,000 people had probably been killed, and approximately 50,000 tortured in as many as 800 prison camps and detention centres in Bosnia. At present, the total number of fatal casualties has been scaled down to not more than 150,000 for Yugoslavia as a whole, with over 100,000 victims in Bosnia alone.

According to the latest data from the Research and Documentation Center in Sarajevo, as well as the demographic expertise of the office of the Prosecutor of the International Criminal Tribunal for the former Yugoslavia (ICTY), of the roughly 1.89 million Muslim Bosnians, over 60,000 died. Of the 1.36 million Serbs in Bosnia, around 25,000 died, and of the Croat population, almost 8,000 died. In terms of absolute numbers the Muslim Bosnians suffered the most: they lost more than twice as many people as the Serbs, and almost eight times as many as the Croats.

Overall it seems that almost as many civilians were killed as combatants. Although men from all three sides were guilty of raping women from the 'enemy group(s)', it was only on the Serbian side that the rape of Muslim women appears to have been a sustained tactic of war and 'ethnic cleansing'.[5]

5.1 Refugees

One-half of the total pre-war population of Bosnia and Herzegovina became uprooted and displaced in one way or another. For the Muslims in Bosnia, the total figure for refugees amounts to around 60%. It is impossible to say how many people fled before their communities were actually attacked, how many fled, or were forced to flee, immediately after being attacked,

Detainees in the Manjača Camp, near Banja Luka, Bosnia and Herzegovina
Source: ICTY

and how many were forced out later. Fleeing before the communities were actually attacked has been called 'ethnic self-cleansing'. In this respect it should be emphasised that hardly any refugees in Yugoslavia left their homes voluntarily.

Some conclusions can be drawn. Firstly, all parties to the conflict suffered very serious losses of live, property, and goods. Secondly, they all, albeit in different ways, contributed to the developments that led to the war, and as part of their actual warfare they all committed various genocidal atrocities and massacres. It follows, thirdly, that in this conflict there is no single side, party, ethnic or population group that can be predominantly considered as 'the perpetrators', or as 'the victims'. On the contrary: within every ethnic category involved there are perpetrators as well as victims. However, this does not imply that all sides are equally responsible and to blame. The actual warfare was started by Bosnian Serbs, with decisive military aid from Serbia proper, and Serbian troops committed a far greater number of war crimes than any of the other parties involved in the conflict.

One of the worst atrocities of the war took place between 6 and 16 July 1995, when the Bosnian Serb Army, under the political leadership of Radovan Karadzic and the military command of Ratko Mladić, captured the formerly 'safe area' of the small town of Srebrenica. Tens of thousands of Muslim Bosnians had taken refuge there from 'ethnic cleansing' elsewhere in the region, and the area was formally protected by a small and insufficiently armed battalion of Dutch UN-soldiers (around 370 peacekeepers). The Dutch UN-soldiers did not — and could not — prevent the Serbs from occupying the area. They did not receive the repeatedly requested and promised close air support which might have stopped the Serbian attack. After capturing the area, the Bosnian Serb Army separated the Muslim men from the women and children. These latter were removed from the area on lorries and buses and taken to territory held by the Bosnian government. The men were taken elsewhere and subsequently executed, for the most part between 13 and 15 July. More than 7,000 Muslim men were deliberately killed in mass shootings.

It took some time for the news about the mass executions to reach the rest of the world. It took even longer for the world to realise that this had been a clear case of genocide by the Bosnian Serb Army. In August 1995 the international community at last resolved that firmer action should be taken against the Serbs by the US, NATO and UN. The horrible massacres near Srebrenica certainly contributed to this decision. From the end of August, Serb targets around Sarajevo and elsewhere in Bosnia were systematically bombed by NATO planes. This forced the Bosnian Serbs and the leadership in Serbia proper to retreat, accept peace negotiations and come to an agreement to end the war.

6.   The ICTY and the Dayton Peace Accords

For nearly three years the international community, represented by the UN, more or less turned a blind eye to the war and the atrocities being committed in Bosnia and Herzegovina. The UN limited itself to weak interventions: endless international negotiations, an arms embargo and some humanitarian aid. UN Peacekeeping ground troops had a strictly limited mandate.

However, journalists made courageous efforts to inform the world about the mass atrocities taking place in Yugoslavia. They visited Serb-run concentration camps, reported on the appalling conditions and treatment of Croat and Muslim detainees, and investigated other war atrocities. Under public pressure, the UN eventually took up its responsibility to investigate war crimes, crimes against humanity, and genocide in Yugoslavia. In February 1993, the Security Council established the International Criminal Tribunal for the former Yugoslavia (ICTY), to be located in The Hague. The ICTY was the first international criminal court since the Nuremberg trials in the aftermath of World War II. Its prosecutors issued indictments against more than 160 suspects, including most of the main figures responsible for the Yugoslav catastrophe. Slobodan Milošević was the first head of state to be put on trial, accused of war crimes and genocide. He died before the verdict was passed. With the recent arrests and trials of Karadzic and Mladić it may yet be

Karadzic on trial at the ICTY
Source: ICTY

that those who ordered the mass killings at Srebrenica will finally be judged.

The war itself ended in late 1995 when all the parties concerned agreed to the Dayton Peace Accords, under pressure from the US and the international community. The Dayton Peace Accords form the foundation of the present state of Bosnia and Herzegovina, which consists of two entities, the Bosnian Serb Republic on 49% of the territory and a combined Croat and Bosnian Muslim entity on the remaining 51%.

The Yugoslavian drama resulted in poor overall living conditions for the large majority of the population and for many people they are far worse than they were around 1985. The destruction of the old federation has led to the formation of seven new states — Slovenia, Croatia, Serbia, Montenegro, Macedonia and Kosovo — and one deeply divided territory, the state of Bosnia and Herzegovina. The violence may have ended but the peace is under pressure, as both entities are run by mainly nationalist politicians who are in continuous conflict and competition. After sixteen years of peace, the future of Bosnia and Herzegovina is still bleak.

Up To $5 Million Reward

Wanted

For crimes against humanity

Slobodan Milosevic
President of the Federal
Republic of Yugoslavia

For genocide and crimes against humanity

Radovan Karadzic   **Ratko Mladic**

Milosevic, Karadzic, and **Mladic** have been indicted by the United Nations International Criminal Tribunal for the Former Yugoslavia for crimes against humanity, including murders and rapes of thousands of innocent civilians, torture, hostage-taking of peacekeepers, wanton destruction of private property, and the destruction of sacred places. **Mladic** and **Karadzic** also have been indicted for genocide.

To bring **Milosevic, Karadzic,** and **Mladic** to justice, the United States Government is offering a reward of up to $5 million for information leading to the transfer to, or conviction by, the International Criminal Tribunal for the Former Yugoslavia of any of these individuals or any other person indicted by the International Tribunal.

If you believe you have information, please contact the nearest U.S. embassy or consulate, or write the U.S. Department of State, Diplomatic Security Service at:

REWARDS FOR JUSTICE
Post Office Box 96781 • Washington, D.C. 20090-6781 U.S.A.
email: mail@dssrewards.net • www.dssrewards.net
1-800-437-6371 (U.S.A. Only)

Wanted for crimes against humanity — 5 million dollar Reward
Source: ICTY

Damage done

At the time of the second Croatian military offensive against Serbian enclaves in Croatia in August 1995, television images were broadcast of fleeing Serbian civilians. One of these showed a Serbian peasant family in flight, the father grim-faced at the wheel of his tractor, pulling a wagon containing a few visibly anxious women and children, and some household goods. They were speeding down a narrow road along a forest. Standing in front of her house at the side of the road an outraged middle-aged Croatian woman shouted abuse at the top of her voice and threw big stones at the passing refugees. These images perhaps symbolise the greatest damage of all: instead of the formerly multi-ethnic and multi-cultural Yugoslavia in which people could move about more or less freely, most of them are now locked up in their own ethnic-national groups and small territories, hemmed in on all sides by borders and frontiers, with bitter memories, and frequently still fearing and hating each other. It will take generations for that damage to be repaired.

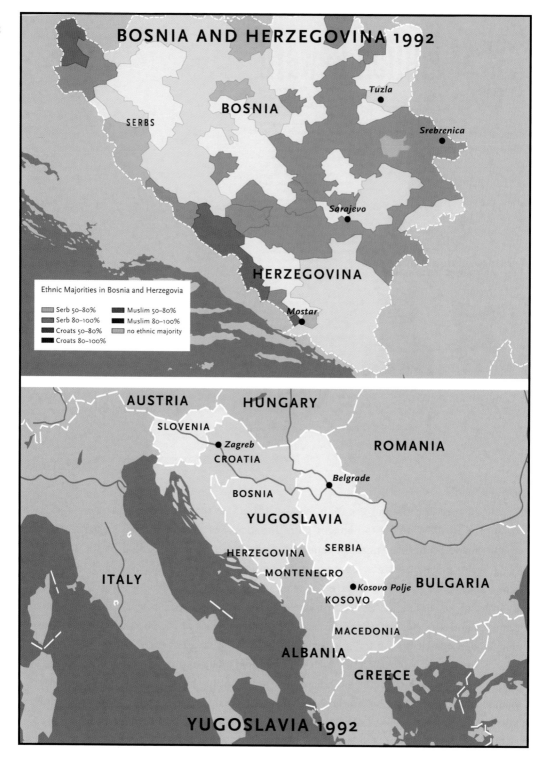

BOSNIA AND HERZEGOVINA 1992

BOSNIA

Tuzla

SERBS

Srebrenica

Sarajevo

HERZEGOVINA

Ethnic Majorities in Bosnia and Herzegovia

- Serb 50–80%
- Serb 80–100%
- Croats 50–80%
- Croats 80–100%
- Muslim 50–80%
- Muslim 80–100%
- no ethnic majority

Mostar

AUSTRIA HUNGARY

SLOVENIA

Zagreb

CROATIA

ROMANIA

Belgrade

BOSNIA

YUGOSLAVIA

HERZEGOVINA

SERBIA

ITALY

MONTENEGRO

Kosovo Polje

BULGARIA

KOSOVO

MACEDONIA

ALBANIA

GREECE

YUGOSLAVIA 1992

Alija Izetbegovic (1925-2003)
President of Bosnia and Herzegovina. Bosnia and Herzegovina was proclaimed an independent state by its government under President Izetbegovic in the early weeks of March 1992. Soon after, fighting broke out in and around the capital Sarajevo. This war lasted for three and a half years, until November 1995.

Radovan Karadžić (b. 1945)
Leader of Bosnian Serbs. Under his political leadership and the military command of Ratko Mladić, the Bosnian Serb Army captured the formerly 'safe area' of the small town of Srebrenica.

Slobodan Milošević (1941-2006)
President of Serbia (1989-1997) and Federal Republic of Yugoslavia (1997-2000). Indicted by the International Criminal Tribunal for the former Yugoslavia for crimes committed in Croatia, Bosnia and Herzegovina and Kosovo. He was put on trial after his deposal in 2000, and died in The Hague in 2006.

Ratko Mladić (b. 1942)
Military commander of Bosnian Serbs. Under the political leadership of Karadžić and the military command of Mladić, the Bosnian Serb Army captured the formerly 'safe area' of the small town of Srebrenica.

Josip Broz Tito (1892-1980)
After the Second World War the federal state of Yugoslavia was created, with the Partisan leader, Josip Broz Tito as the head of state. After the death of Tito in 1980 a power vacuum ensued.

Franjo Tuđman (1922-1999)
Military historian, founder and head of the nationalist HDZ Croatian Democratic Union, Hrvatska Demokratska Zajednica. President of Croatia in the 1990s.

Glossary

Chetniks	Serbian nationalists, responsible for many mass killings.
Ethnic cleansing	A purposeful policy designed by one ethnic or religious group to remove by violent and terror-inspiring means the civilian population of another ethnic or religious group from certain geographic areas. To a large extent, it is carried out in the name of misguided nationalism, historic grievances and a powerful driving sense of revenge.[6]
Ethnic nationalism	'Ethnic nationalism is an attempt to maintain or to recreate a sense of identity and community in the face of the threat of cultural assimilation or annihilation.'[7] Under the leadership of Tuđman, ethnic nationalism was no longer restrained.
ICTY	The International Criminal Tribunal for the former Yugoslavia.
JNA	The People's Army (*Jugoslovenska Narodna Armija*). The JNA contained around 70,000 officers, approximately 70% of whom were Serbs and Montenegrins. The great majority of the officer corps considered the JNA predominantly as the national guardian of the Yugoslav federation and of party communism.
TO	Parallel to the People's Army, a semi-military organisation was set up, the so-called territorial defence forces (*Teritorijalna Odbrana*). These forces were organised per republic and each consisted of several tens of thousands of workers, peasants, and civilians. Trained and equipped, they could mobilise quickly in case of enemy attack and could then operate as guerrilla troops.
Ustaša	Croatian fascist movement launched genocidal campaigns against Serbs and Jews and were notorious for killing Serbs, Jews, Gypsies, Communists, and political opponents.
Yugoslavia	Six republics which formed the federal state — Slovenia, Croatia, Bosnia and Herzegovina, Serbia, Montenegro, and Macedonia — existed in the western part of the Balkans during the 20th century.

Timeline

1400	
1500	**15th century:** The Ottoman Empire conquered a large part of the Balkans — including Macedonia, Serbia, parts of Montenegro, and Bosnia and Herzegovina — but ultimately not Croatia and Slovenia, which became part of the Austro-Hungarian Empire.
1918	
1941	
1945	**1918:** After the First World War Yugoslavia, the Kingdom of Serbs, Croats and Slovenes was established.
1980	
1991	**1941-1945:** During the Second World War the country was occupied, mainly by Germany and Italy, and was deeply divided, which caused very differentiated memories of this time. Croat fascists (Ustaše), Serbian Chetniks and Communist Partisans fought each other and committed many mass atrocities.
1992	**1980:** Ethnic nationalism began to rise among different nationalities and in different regions.
1993	**25 June 1991:** The Republics of Slovenia and Croatia declared its independence. The Ten Day War with Yugoslavia followed.
1994	**1991-1995:** Croatian War of Independence.
1995	**1992-1995:** War in Bosnia and Herzegovina.
1996	**May 1993:** The Security Council established the International Criminal Tribunal for the former Yugoslavia (ICTY), to be located in The Hague.

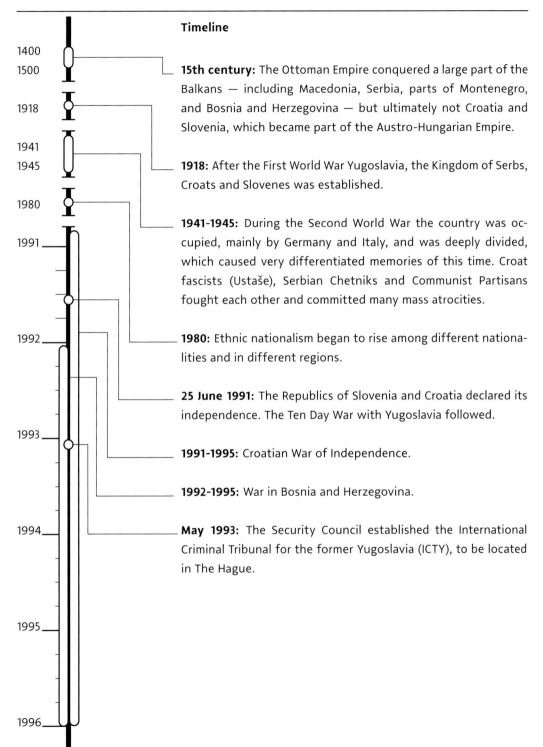

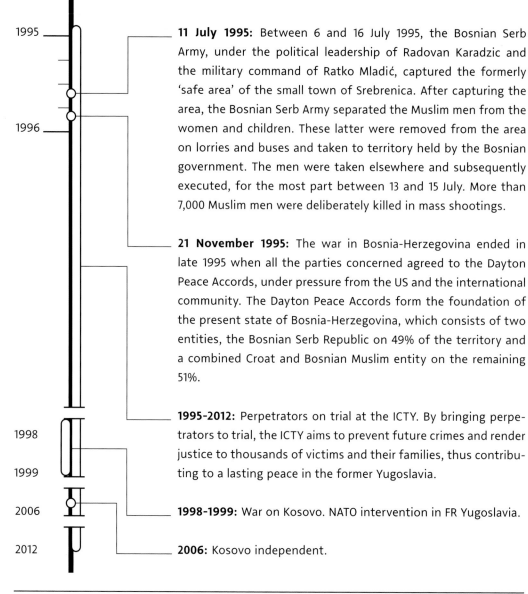

1995

1996

1998

1999

2006

2012

11 July 1995: Between 6 and 16 July 1995, the Bosnian Serb Army, under the political leadership of Radovan Karadzic and the military command of Ratko Mladić, captured the formerly 'safe area' of the small town of Srebrenica. After capturing the area, the Bosnian Serb Army separated the Muslim men from the women and children. These latter were removed from the area on lorries and buses and taken to territory held by the Bosnian government. The men were taken elsewhere and subsequently executed, for the most part between 13 and 15 July. More than 7,000 Muslim men were deliberately killed in mass shootings.

21 November 1995: The war in Bosnia-Herzegovina ended in late 1995 when all the parties concerned agreed to the Dayton Peace Accords, under pressure from the US and the international community. The Dayton Peace Accords form the foundation of the present state of Bosnia-Herzegovina, which consists of two entities, the Bosnian Serb Republic on 49% of the territory and a combined Croat and Bosnian Muslim entity on the remaining 51%.

1995-2012: Perpetrators on trial at the ICTY. By bringing perpetrators to trial, the ICTY aims to prevent future crimes and render justice to thousands of victims and their families, thus contributing to a lasting peace in the former Yugoslavia.

1998-1999: War on Kosovo. NATO intervention in FR Yugoslavia.

2006: Kosovo independent.

Notes

1 Filipovic, Z. (1994). *Zlata's Diary. A child's life in Sara-jevo*. London.

2 Polonsky, A. (1975). *The Little Dictators. The History of Eastern Europe since 1918*. Londen: Routledge & Kegan Paul, pp. 94-106; Skocpol, T. (1979). *States and Social Revolutions*. Cambridge, pp. 24-33.

3 http://www.balkandevelopment.org/edu_bos.html.

4 LeBor, A. (2002). *Milosevic. A biography*. London, pp. 79-82.

5 Tabeau, E., *War-related Deaths in the 1992-1995 Armed Conflicts in Bosnia and Herzegovina: A Critique of Previous Estimates and Recent Results*.

6 Report of the Commission of Experts Established Pursuant to United Nations Security Council Resolution 780 (1992), 27 May 1994 (S/1994/674), English p. 33.

7 Danforth, L.M. (1995). *The Macedonian conflict: ethnic nationalism in a transnational world*. New Yersey, pp. 11-12..

Sonderausgabe

Preis 15 Pfg.

Süddeutsche Zeitung

MÜNCHNER NACHRICHTEN AUS POLITIK · KULTUR · WIRTSCHAFT UND SPORT

München, Dienstag, 1. Oktober 1946

Göring: zum Tode

Heß: lebenslänglich

Ribbentrop: zum Tode

Keitel: zum Tode

Kaltenbrunner: zum Tode

Rosenberg: zum Tode

Frank: zum Tode

Frick: zum Tode

Die Sühne der Hauptkriegsverbrecher

Das Urteil in Nürnberg

12 Todesurteile
Schacht, Papen und Fritzsche freigesprochen

Nürnberg, 1. Oktober (SZ, Dana)

In der Dienstagnachmittag-Verhandlung um 15.55 Uhr gab das Nürnberger Oberste Militärgericht das Urteil gegen die einzelnen Hauptangeklagten bekannt, das von der ganzen Welt mit ungeheurer Spannung erwartet wurde und den Schlußstein setzt unter eine Bilanz von Völkermord und Verbrechen furchtbaren Ausmaßes. Lordrichter Lawrence verkündete folgendes Strafmaß:

Zum Tode verurteilt:

Göring:	Tod durch Strang
Ribbentrop:	Tod durch Strang
Keitel:	Tod durch Strang
Kaltenbrunner:	Tod durch Strang
Rosenberg:	Tod durch Strang
Frank:	Tod durch Strang
Frick:	Tod durch Strang
Streicher:	Tod durch Strang
Sauckel:	Tod durch Strang
Jodl:	Tod durch Strang
Seyß-Inquart:	Tod durch Strang

Schacht:	nicht schuldig nach allen Anklagepunkten, sofortige Entlassung nach Ende der Verhandlung angeordnet.
Papen:	nicht schuldig nach allen Anklagepunkten, sofortige Entlassung nach Ende der Verhandlung angeordnet.
Fritzsche:	nicht schuldig nach allen Anklagepunkten, sofortige Entlassung nach Ende der Verhandlung angeordnet.

In Abwesenheit:

Bormann:	zum Tode durch den Strang verurteilt.

Lebenslänglich Gefängnis:

Heß:	lebenslängliches Gefängnis
Funk:	lebenslängliches Gefängnis
Raeder:	lebenslängliches Gefängnis

Gefängnisstrafen:

Dönitz:	zehn Jahre Gefängnis
Neurath:	fünfzehn Jahre Gefängnis
Schirach:	zwanzig Jahre Gefängnis
Speer:	zwanzig Jahre Gefängnis

Letzte Meldung:

Die sowjetische Delegation weicht von der Entscheidung des Gerichts ab, Schacht, Papen und Fritzsche freizusprechen, und fordert, daß die drei Angeklagten hätten verurteilt werden müssen.

Ebenso weicht die sowjetische Delegation von dem lebenslänglichen Gefängnisurteil gegen Heß ab, der zum Tode hätte verurteilt werden sollen.

Weiter hätten OKW, Generalstab und Reichskabinett, nach der Meinung der sowjetischen Richter als verbrecherische Organisationen verurteilt werden sollen.

„Im Namen der Gerechtigkeit"

(SZ) Eine Herausforderung an die ganze Welt und alles, was Menschenantlitz trägt — an alles aus, was in dieser Welt als Name zur Geltung und der Rechte Gültigkeit hatte, ist in Nürnberg mit einem Rechtsspruch beantwortet worden, der nicht nur Schuldige aburteilt, sondern darüber hinaus für die ganze Welt zugleich auch ihren Recht neu feststellt und verankert.

Der Begriff „Völkermord" hat eine neue, tiefere Bedeutung bekommen! Gegen die in der Geschichte beispiellose Vergewaltigung aller der Prinzipien und Maßstäbe, die das Leben der Menschen und Völker bestimmten, haben die Männer, die in Nürnberg im Gericht gesessen und geurteilt haben, vor den Augen der Welt statuiert, daß derjenige zum Verbrecher wird, der sich gegen die Gesetze der Menschenordnung vergeht. Mögen diese Gesetze geschrieben oder ungeschrieben sein, — sie müssen „heilige" Gesetz sein und bleiben, wenn nicht die ganze positive Welt untergehen soll.

Aus dieser Verantwortung der Menschheit gegenüber darf es im Zusammenleben der Völker keine Flucht geben, — und kein noch immer formulierte Begründung darf für die Verfolgung dieser Verbrecher-Entschuldigung bedeuten, wenn es nicht das Zusammenleben der Menschen und Völker der Willkür preisgeben. Kein Befehl oder Eid darf je in der Welt als Entschuldigung dafür gelten, daß solche Verbrechen und solche Rechtsbruch gibt es keine Rechtsgültige! Befehlsgewalt verbrecherisch gehandelt zu haben, ist kein mildernder Umstand.

Nichts wäre verfehlter, als das Nürnberger Gerichtsverfahren dahin interpretieren zu wollen, es habe sich dabei darum gehandelt, die paar Massenmörder und Großverbrecher abzuurteilen und sie zu hängen. Der Mord an ganzen Völkern und Rassen und millionenfache Vernichtung menschlicher Leben sind eine so ungeheuerliche Kette grauenhafter Verbrechen, daß der Tod einiger Menschen dagegenüber fast belanglos erscheint. Auch macht die Beseitigung einiger Verantwortlicher nichts ungeschehen. Der deutsche Anstand, der den Mißtrauen ins KZ gebracht ist, wird nicht lebendig; die Erniedrigung und das Leid, und der unermeßliche Tod, der auch nur einen einzigen Juden getan worden ist, wird nie wieder

(Fortsetzung auf Seite 2)

Funk: lebenslänglich

Streicher: zum Tode

Schacht: nicht schuldig

Raeder: lebenslänglich

Schirach: Zwanzig Jahre

Sauckel: zum Tode

Jodl: zum Tode

Papen: nicht schuldig

Seyß-Inquart: zum Tode

Speer: Zwanzig Jahre

Dönitz: zehn Jahre

Neurath: Fünfzehn Jahre

Fritzsche: nicht schuldig

Bormann: zum Tode

'Das Urteil in Nürnberg'
Source: Museen der stadt Nürnberg Dokumentationszentrum Reichsparteitagsgelände

The Crime of Genocide and International Law

Martin Mennecke

Introduction

War crimes, crimes against humanity, aggression and genocide — international law recognises many international crimes. None of these, however, attract the same attention as genocide does. When allegations of genocide are raised, the world pricks up its ears. Using the term genocide can have far-reaching implications.

1. The historical background

Genocide is not a new phenomenon. Even classical writings recount instances of mass killings, and the colonial era witnessed numerous cases of genocidal violence both in North and Latin America as well as in Africa. The Holocaust was neither the first nor the last genocide.

Nonetheless, it was the extermination of the European Jews that gave rise to international law defining and prohibiting the crime of genocide. In 1944, the Polish lawyer Raphael Lemkin created the very term 'genocide', joining the Greek word 'genos' (race, nation or tribe) and the Latin suffix 'cide' (from 'caedere', to kill). Lemkin had managed to escape the Holocaust via Sweden before reaching the United States where he published *Axis Rule in Occupied Europe*, a detailed account of the occupation regime imposed by Nazi Germany.

Genocide according to Lemkin

In this book, *Axis Rule in Occupied Europe,* Lemkin introduced the concept of genocide, defining it as: 'the destruction of a nation or of an ethnic group [...] a coordinated plan of different actions aiming at the destruction of essential foundations of the life of national groups, with the aim of annihilating the groups themselves. The objectives of such a plan would be disintegration of the political and social institutions, of culture, language, national feelings, religion, and the economic existence of national groups, and the destruction of the personal security, liberty, health, dignity, and even the lives of the individuals belonging to such groups. Genocide is directed against the national group as an entity, and the actions involved are directed against individuals, not in their individual capacity, but as members of the national group.'

Dr. Raphael Lemkin, 12 September 1948
Source: United Nations

Lemkin's work was clearly motivated by his personal experience of the war and the Holocaust, including the loss of dozens of family members. However Lemkin also built on his earlier work concerning atrocities committed against the Armenians and in various European colonies.

Nuremberg War Crime Trial

In 1945 and 1946 the triumphant allied forces installed the International Military Tribunal at the German city of Nuremberg. Here some of the most important captured Nazi suspects were tried and in most cases convicted. Among them were Hermann Göring, Arthur Seyss-Inquart, Albert Speer and Joachim von Ribbentrop. Adolf Hitler, Joseph Goebbels and Heinrich Himmler were not tried because they had committed suicide at the end of the war.

At the Nuremberg trial, the new concept of genocide did not play any significant role. As a matter of fact, genocide was not incorporated into the rules establishing the Nuremberg Tribunal that was to hear the cases against the political and military leadership of Nazi Germany. This was in part due to the fact that Lemkin's invention of the term 'genocide' did not yet exist under international law. Immediately after the war, the attention did not centre on the policy of extermination, but on Nazi Germany's wars of aggression which were referred to as 'the supreme crime'. Lemkin was not pleased with this. He had personally travelled to Nuremberg to lobby for the inclusion of genocide charges into the proceedings, but to no avail. Lemkin redirected his efforts towards lobbying the newly founded United Nations to adopt a legal

Nuremberg War Crime Trial, defendants dock
Source: National Archives and Records Administration

instrument prohibiting genocide — and so it did in 1948, just four years after Lemkin had published his first thoughts on genocide.

At the time, the UN Genocide Convention was considered a milestone. The euphoric assessment of the new genocide treaty was, however, not a sentiment shared by all observers. International law professor Georg Schwarzenberger commented that the 'whole Convention is based on the assumption of virtuous governments and criminal individuals, a reversal of the truth (...) [T]he Convention is unnecessary where it can be applied and inapplicable where it may be necessary. It is an insult to intelligence and dangerous (...) [and will] prove on examination to mark no real advance.'

Today, we know that the critics were not totally wrong. The pledge given in the preamble of the Genocide Convention 'to liberate mankind from such an odious scourge' in order to avoid for the future such 'great losses on humanity', this pledge has not been realised. Instead the period after 1948 also saw numerous instances of genocidal violence, turning the 20th century into what some have called the 'century of genocide.' The writer David Rieff therefore once quipped that the pledge of 'never again' only could be understood to mean 'never again will Germans kill Jews in Europe'.

2. The UN Genocide Convention on the Prevention and Punishment of the Crime of Genocide

The UN Genocide Convention was adopted by the UN General Assembly on 9 December 1948, one day after the Universal Declaration of Human Rights was passed by the same forum. The treaty was drafted and negotiated under the auspices of the United Nations — therefore the reference to the UN in the title of the instrument — but is otherwise an independent international treaty among states and not linked to the United Nations as such. As with all international treaties, the Genocide Convention only became a binding legal instrument once a sufficient number of states had formally agreed to be bound by this new treaty. This was the case on 12 January 1951 and since then, the Genocide Convention has been in force and applies to its member states. This means that crimes committed prior to 1951 cannot be legally prosecuted under the Genocide Convention. This is true, for example, for both the Armenian mass killings, the murderous persecution of the Sinti and Roma and the Holocaust. That being said, one can of course still apply the label 'genocide' to these and other crimes outside the courtroom.

Today the UN Genocide Convention counts 142 member states. This means that more than 50 states have not yet ratified the Genocide Convention, including states such as Somalia and Japan. This does not mean, however, that these states can commit genocide without violating international law. Instead these states are bound by what is called customary international law, building on the long-standing general practice and legal opinion of the international community of states pursuant to which genocide is a crime under international law. This has been confirmed in numerous international judgements. Indeed, the prohibition of genocide is said to enjoy *jus cogens* status.

Jus cogens

This is a Latin term meaning 'compelling law'. It refers to a special category of international law norms which are considered to be peremptory so that no state can legally deviate from them. Other norms with a *jus cogens* status include the prohibition of slavery and the prohibition of torture. International law does not explicitly regulate, however, what the consequences of a violation of a *jus cogens* norm are.

2.1 Provisions

The UN Genocide Convention consists of nineteen provisions. The Convention outlines how member states are to deal with the crime of genocide and puts great emphasis on how to punish it, including several provisions that refer to criminal law and the accountability of individuals. At the same time the Genocide Convention could be characterised as a human rights

instrument, as it sets out to protect the right of existence of certain groups listed in the treaty.
Finally, the Genocide Convention also deals with states and their responsibilities, as it concerns their options and duties as regards the prevention and punishment of the crime of genocide. The UN Genocide Convention is thus an international treaty that both deals with human rights issues, questions of criminal law and state responsibility.

Turning to specific provisions of the Genocide Convention, Article 1 stipulates that member states 'undertake to prevent and punish the crime of genocide'. In Article 2 the treaty defines the crime of genocide. Remarkably, the Genocide Convention does not establish any specific institutions such as a court or a committee to supervise the implementation of the aforementioned duties. Article 6 refers to an international penal tribunal, but the treaty stops short of establishing it — reflecting the lack of political will to do so at the time of the treaty's drafting. In Article 9 the Genocide Convention refers to an actual tool to address genocide: state parties to the treaty can take disputes with other member states concerning the Convention to the International Court of Justice (ICJ). This court does not deal with questions of individual criminal accountability, but settles inter-state disputes. In practice, however, this reference to the ICJ has not resulted into very many cases.

3. The definition of genocide under international law

The body of scholarly literature on genocide contains an abundance of definitions of genocide. Many genocide scholars present their own, personal definition of genocide, and that leads to different cases being included in the discussion. In international law, things are in a sense more simple as regards what is genocide: there is only one definition and that has been the same ever since the UN Genocide Convention was adopted in 1948. Governments have had numerous opportunities to amend the original definition to address any shortcomings or new developments — but never have done so. As late as in 1998, on the 50th anniversary of the Genocide Convention, states decided to use the original definition word by word when drafting the treaty establishing the new International Criminal Court. This is interesting to note because one of the reasons that genocide scholars keep on designing new definitions is that the legal definition has been widely criticised ever since its adoption.

Definition

In the present Convention, genocide means any of the following acts committed with the intent to destroy, in whole or in part, a national, ethnical, racial or religious group, as such:

(a) Killing members of the group;

(b) Causing serious bodily or mental harm to members of the group;

(c) Deliberately inflicting on the group conditions of life calculated to bring about its physical destruction in whole or in part;

(d) Imposing measures intended to prevent births within the group;

(e) Forcibly transferring children of the group to another group.

3.1 Intent

A first reading of the definition allows us to make several important observations. First, the definition is composed of two equally important parts describing respectively the perpetrator's intent and then the actions (in letters a-e) that can constitute genocide. Concerning the perpetrator's intent, the definition requires a very specific intent, i.e. the intent to focus on destroying one of the protected groups and not merely the intent to commit one of the genocidal acts. The question is thus not only whether the perpetrator wanted to kill an individual person — but whether he or she did so intending to destroy the group the victims belonged to.

This form of intent is difficult to prove; in court proceedings, judges often infer the intent from the actual events on the ground, for example from speeches or writings authored by the perpetrator. Only if both requirements, including the special intent, are met in a given situation, can one conclude genocide has been committed in terms of international law.

Secondly, and quite different from what one might expect, the legal definition of genocide includes under relevant acts not only 'killing', but also other forms of conduct including, for example, the forcible transfer of children. It is important to note that legally speaking genocide does not require mass killings or gas chambers, but can be committed in different ways — it all depends on whether the perpetrator has the requisite intent.

Thirdly, the legal definition of genocide only protects certain groups against destruction, i.e. national, religious, racial and ethnic groups. This listing is not open-ended or exemplary — there are these four groups, no more.

Fourthly, the legal definition does not define genocide as the total annihilation of a group, but makes it a crime to intend to destroy any of these groups in whole or *in part*. Thus even a brief first survey shows that genocide under international law is quite different from how the layman might define it.

4. Difficulties in practice

Two international tribunals have, in the cases concerning the war in the Former Yugoslavia and the Rwandan genocide, applied the legal definition of genocide and shed more light on its scope and meaning. There are two aspects which deserve our particular attention. As stated, the genocide definition provided by the UN Genocide Convention only protects four specified groups. This has been widely criticised as being too limited and arbitrary, but it can only be changed by those making international law, i.e. states. The work of the tribunals identified another issue: who exactly is protected as a 'national, ethnic, racial and religious group'? Scrutinising the Rwandan genocide it all of a sudden appeared that the two prevalent groups — the Tutsi and the Hutu — spoke the same language, shared the same customs and were both Christian. How could the victims then be a distinct 'ethnic' group? It took the judges of the relevant tribunal, the International Criminal Tribunal for Rwanda, several years to work out a convincing answer. Now it is generally accepted that the question is not whether the victim group lives up to some abstract definition for ethnic groups taken from an encyclopaedia, but whether the perpetrators have perceived the victims as members of a distinct ethnic, racial etc. group.

Another important question facing the international tribunals was what to make of the definition's reference to destroying the group 'in whole or *in part.*' The legal definition of genocide is focused on the perpetrator's intent, not on the success of his or her actions — in other words, for any determination of genocide it is not necessary that the whole victim group has been exterminated. As for the meaning of the 'in part' segment, the international case law found that there is no minimum number of victims. Instead, the phrase 'in part' involves two considerations, which might be seen as 'qualitative' and 'quantitative'. As for the latter, the tribunals have held that the perpetrator must have aimed at a 'substantial' part of the victim group, i.e. a considerable number of individuals. As for 'quality', the question to ask is whether the perpetrator aimed at a 'significant part' of the group, such as for example its leadership or all the women. This intent can also be focused on a certain geographically limited area. How exactly to apply the 'in part' segment, however, remains under discussion.

There are more such difficult questions. For example, in one of the early judgements concerning the Rwandan genocide, the judges held that rape can form part of genocidal violence. This was a remarkable holding, as sexual violence hitherto had not been given much prominence in international criminal law. Consequently, the judgement was celebrated by many as an overdue recognition of the suffering of women during genocides. On first sight the decision makes immediate sense, as rape obviously causes the victim both mental and physical harm. On further thought, however, the question arises whether the perpetrator indeed commits the rape with the intent to destroy the relevant group as such — as required by the legal definition. It is notable that since the first seminal decision classifying rape as genocide there has been very little follow-up in subsequent judgements. Many genocide scholars include sexual violence into their discussions of genocide, but there is still significant room for clarification when applying the legal definition.

> Case No. ICTR-96-4-T, the prosecutor v. Jean-Paul Akayesu, Judgement on 2 September 1998:
>
> With regard, particularly, to the acts described in paragraphs 12(A) and 12(B) of the Indictment, that is, rape and sexual violence, the Chamber wishes to underscore the fact that in its opinion, they constitute genocide in the same way as any other act as long as they were committed with the specific intent to destroy, in whole or in part, a particular group, targeted as such. Indeed, rape and sexual violence certainly constitute infliction of serious physical and mental harm on the victims and are even, according to the Chamber,

one of the worst ways of inflicting harm on the victim as he or she suffers both physical and mental harm. In light of all the evidence before it, the Chamber is satisfied that the acts of rape and sexual violence described above, were committed solely against Tutsi women, many of whom were subjected to the worst public humiliation, mutilated, and raped several times, often in public, in the Bureau Communal premises or in other public places, and often by more than one assailant. These rapes resulted in physical and psychological destruction of Tutsi women, their families and their communities. Sexual violence was an integral part of the process of destruction, specifically targeting Tutsi women and specifically contributing to their destruction and to the destruction of the Tutsi group as a whole.

4.1 Cultural genocide and international law

In the non-legal literature on genocide much has been written on how the forceful suppression of traditional languages and customs can lead to the extinction of a given culture — an experience shared by many indigenous people. Under international law, however, the prevalent view is that cultural genocide cannot be squared with the legal definition of genocide, as the phrase 'intent to destroy' is understood to focus on the *physical* destruction of a group, not its culture. Acts that could be considered 'cultural genocide' are therefore only included in the legal proceedings when they can help to establish the intent of the perpetrator to physically destroy a group. It could, however, be asked whether this indeed is the only possible reading of the Genocide Convention — perhaps the phrase 'intent to destroy' could also accommodate cultural genocide, as the definition itself does not explicitly refer to *physical* destruction.

5. Genocide scholars and the legal definition of genocide

Overall, the legal definition has shown that it is far more flexible and open for new interpretations than many of its critics had believed. This notwithstanding, many genocide scholars remain critical of the legal definition of genocide. While some of their long-standing criticisms have been addressed in the case law, certain issues remain inherent in the legal definition as it stands.

First of all, many genocide scholars argue that the intent requirement sets too high a threshold, as it is difficult to prove whether, for example, a perpetrator by killing members of a group and persecuting others also intended to destroy the group as such. This issue often arises when discussing campaigns of what has been dubbed 'ethnic cleansing'. This term describes scenarios where the perpetrator forces another ethnic group to leave their home territory by committing atrocities against members of the group without, though, exterminating the group as such. A relevant example is the war in the former Yugoslavia in the 1990s, when the Bosnian Muslims became the victims of large scale 'ethnic cleansing' — a series of crimes which many victims as well as non-legal scholars described as genocide, while the majority of international lawyers and eventually international tribunals held that the requisite genocidal intent to destroy the group of Bosnian Muslims was lacking. This discussion touches on the essence of the question of what is genocide — and the legal definition gives a narrower answer to the question than may be agreeable to victims and scholars — but for lawyers, the definition has to be applied as it stands.

Another bone of contention is the number of groups protected under the UN Genocide Convention. The legal definition only protects four specific groups — no more. This is for historic reasons; at the time of the drafting there were also other versions on the table, including a definition that would have protected social and political groups. In the end, the Soviet Union and other states succeeded at removing political groups from the definition, a move consented to by the other governments in order to secure a final text acceptable to the largest number of states possible. As a result, a regime can turn against its political opposition and kill each single member of that group — without committing genocide. A relevant example can be seen in Cambodia where the crimes committed by the Khmer Rouge only in part meet the requirements of the legal definition: a minority of the victims was killed because of their membership of a specific ethnic or religious group; by far the largest group of victims belonged to a social segment of the society — but social groups are not protected by the Genocide Convention. Of course, such a policy could still be prosecuted under international law, for example as crimes against humanity, but for many observers there is no convincing argument why these killings should not be classified as genocide, as they concern the purposeful destruction of a group. States have decided not to act on this criticism; under international law only the four aforementioned groups remain protected against genocide.

6. To punish the crime of genocide

Notwithstanding all discussions on its exact scope and meaning, the legal definition of genocide first and foremost accomplishes one thing: it defines a crime and establishes the individual accountability of those breaching the prohibition of genocide. In fact, Article 1 of the UN Genocide Convention states that member states to the treaty 'undertake to punish genocide' — in other words, all states ratifying it are under a duty to punish genocide. The Genocide Convention does not set up an international tribunal to implement this duty — it only refers to the future creation of such body.

The Convention's emphasis is rather on the member states and their national judicial systems. The Convention provides in Article 6 that 'persons charged with genocide (...) shall be tried by a competent tribunal of the State in the territory of which the act was committed'. Notably, the Convention thus limits the aforementioned duty to punish to the home state of the perpetrators. By way of example this means that Rwanda as member state to the Genocide Convention is under an obligation to punish the perpetrators of the Rwandan genocide — but the Nether-

ICJ Great Hall of Justice,
5 December 2011
Source: United Nations

lands or France are not with regards to the Rwandan genocide. This limitation to some extent lessens the significance of the duty to punish genocide, as the home state most often also will be the one responsible for the mass atrocities to start with — which in turn reduces the likelihood of actual investigations. Only once there has been a shift of power can one expect domestic trials on genocide as, for example, in Bosnia and Rwanda.

6.1   Universal jurisdiction

A more far-reaching duty to punish genocide — one that would apply regardless of the perpetrator's nationality and the site of the crime — was not agreeable in 1948 and is not included under the Convention. Today, customary international law allows states to prosecute *genocidaires* even when they stem from other countries and have committed the crime elsewhere. While there is still no duty to do so, several countries such as the Netherlands or Germany have enabled their own domestic courts to punish genocide regardless of where it has been committed. This type of prosecution is called universal jurisdiction, as the state's claim of competence to investigate is not based on the perpetrator's nationality (nationality principle) or the crime site (territorial principle), but the specific universal condemnation of the crime as shocking to all mankind (universality principle). Universal jurisdiction cases are not without their critics, as they are sometimes portrayed as Western meddling with the domestic affairs of other countries. Universal jurisdiction cases also entail numerous practical challenges. With regards to the Rwandan genocide for example, a Dutch prosecutor would have to investigate crimes that were committed in a country far away, protect witnesses that are not in the Netherlands and organise translation from the local language Kinyarwanda into Dutch. Proponents of universal jurisdiction cases do acknowledge the difficulties, but respond that under some circumstances these outside interventions are all that is available and thus necessary to overcome impunity

and provide justice to the victims of these crimes. This is particularly true if the genocidal
regime has remained in power or is protected against investigations in the relevant state by
means of an amnesty.

6.2   State responsibility — The International Court of Justice

At the international level, two different systems have to be distinguished: one to hold individuals accountable, and one to focus on the responsibility of states. State responsibility is incurred
when a state violates a norm of international law — such as the prohibition of genocide. The
Genocide Convention allows for such matters to be heard before the International Court of
Justice (ICJ). This court is the highest judicial organ of the United Nations and is situated in The
Hague, the Netherlands. It cannot hear cases concerning individual human rights nor respond
to individual complaints, but only serves as a forum for states to settle inter-state disputes.
The ICJ does not conclude a case by punishing a state, but makes a finding on whether a state
has violated a given rule of international law and whether it should compensate the 'victim'
state for that violation. In regard to genocide there has only been one ICJ case where the court
rendered a judgement on the substance of the matter. This was on 26 February 2007 in a case
initiated by Bosnia and Herzegovina against Serbia. Bosnia won the case in that Serbia was held
to have violated both the duty to punish and to prevent genocide — but the Court also ruled
that Serbia had not herself committed genocide in Bosnia and would not need to compensate
Bosnia. Thus, despite Serbia becoming the very first state since the adoption of the Genocide
Convention to be held in violation of the treaty, the judgement was not received well in Bosnia.

The Secretary-General
addresses the ICTR
Staff, 27 February 2009.
Source: United Nations

6.3 Individual responsibility — international criminal tribunals

There is by now a whole range of international and semi-international tribunals where *individuals* can be prosecuted for violating the prohibition of genocide. To appreciate today's variety of options, it needs to be recalled that it took the international community of states almost half a century from the adoption of the Genocide Convention before it mustered the political will to establish the first tribunal to prosecute individuals guilty of genocide. This happened in 1993 when the UN Security Council established the International Criminal Tribunal for the former Yugoslavia (ICTY) to hold those accountable that were deemed responsible for the massive human rights violations during the then ongoing conflict in the former Yugoslavia. A year later, the Security Council established another tribunal, the International Criminal Tribunal for Rwanda (ICTR), to prosecute those with the greatest responsibility for the Rwandan genocide.

Both tribunals were thus created by the UN Security Council, focused on one certain conflict and were designed to be only temporary in their tasks. The ICTR became the institution to issue the first genocide judgement of any international court when, in 1998, it convicted a Rwandan major by the name of Jean Paul Akayesu for genocide. The ICTR has since heard some 60 additional genocide cases and will have to finish its work by 2013 or 14 because the Security Council has decided so. Conversely, the ICTY has only produced a handful of genocide convictions and all of them concern the mass executions in July 1995, when Bosnian Serbs murdered more than 8,000 Bosnian Muslim boys and men at the town of Srebrenica. The ICTY will also soon have to conclude its work.

6.4 The International Criminal Court

The ICTY and ICTR were ground-breaking and standard-setting with their work and thus paved the way for the realisation of a historic project, the establishment of a *permanent* and *universal* institution to prosecute international crimes. In 1998, after lengthy and controversial negotiations, the drafting of the founding treaty for the International Criminal Court (ICC) was concluded. Surprisingly, only four years later, this treaty had already gained the support of more than 60 states which committed to the goal of ending impunity for genocide and other international crimes, which in turn meant that the Court could become active and start its work on 1 July 2002. Today the court has 120 member states, including all EU members, most Latin American states, more than 30 African states, but not the United States, Russia, China, India or Israel. It also is situated in The Hague, but because of the separate treaty is not a UN organ, but an independent international organisation. The ICC has no police force and thus depends on the political support of its members and can only hear cases against individuals believed to be responsible for genocide or other international crimes if the relevant home state is not able or willing to carry out the investigation or prosecution (the so-called principle of complementarity). The ICC rendered its very first judgement on 14 March 2012. Thomas Lubanga, a rebel leader from the Democratic Republic of Congo, was found guilty of enlisting and using child soldiers.

The Secretary-General addresses Cambodian Courts' Extraordinary Chambers, 27 October 2010.
Source: United Nations

In addition, the Court has issued a number of arrest warrants, including one against the sitting president of Sudan, Omar Al Bashir. The ICC Prosecutor views the ongoing violence in the Darfur province of Sudan as genocide and asserts that Bashir is guilty of genocide. So far Sudan has rejected any cooperation with the Court — but the difference between the ICC and all other international institutions dealing with international crimes is that the ICC is a permanent institution. It can wait. This may not be enough at the time for the victims of genocide — but it keeps genocide and the international promise to punish genocide on the agenda.

6.5   The hybrid tribunal — the ECCC

There is one last mechanism of international justice to be mentioned here and these are the so-called semi-international or hybrid tribunals. Such a tribunal exists for example to look into the crimes committed by the Khmer Rouge in Cambodia in 1975-1979 and is called the Extraordinary Chambers in the Courts of Cambodia (ECCC). In contrast to the ICC, the ECCC is not a purely international, independent organisation, but is placed within the domestic system and in part also staffed by nationals of the relevant state. The potential benefit of this construction was that unlike the ICC, such a hybrid tribunal would be placed close to the victims and the sites where the crimes were committed. This would both be cheaper and more effective. In addition the involvement of domestic staff would allow for the transfer of knowledge and capacity building. The reality of the Cambodian example, however, is that the hybrid tribunal is very vulnerable to political pressure and interference from the home state government, jeopardising the whole effort to hold *genocidaires* accountable.

7.   Punishing *genocidaires*

The Genocide Convention focuses on punishing the crime of genocide — but the question is whether the punishment of the perpetrators indeed always is an option, or even the appropriate, most promising answer. Reading this in the context of the Holocaust, even asking the very question may seem frivolous. Of course *genocidaires* should be punished before a court of law. According to this opinion the question rather ought to be whether any form of punishment ever could be appropriate to respond to the horrors of genocide.

But then there is the case of the Rwandan genocide. In little more than 100 days, in a country of some 8 million people, more than 800,000 Tutsi were slaughtered — almost three quarters of the country's total Tutsi population. This genocide was not committed by means of gas chambers or mass executions; instead most of the killings were done by clubbing, stabbing, and so on. It is believed that several hundred thousand individuals took part in the killings. After the genocide there were only some 40 lawyers left in Rwanda to deal with this — the rest had either been killed or fled the country. To prosecute the perpetrators of the genocide before regular courts in Rwanda would have been an impossible task and literally have taken hundreds of years. At the same time, many Rwandans also questioned whether an exclusive focus on punishment would allow the country to achieve any meaningful reconciliation. After all, the genocide stemmed from an internal struggle for power among the two groups — Tutsi and Hutu — living side by side in the same communities, both prior to and after the genocide.

The complex situation in post-genocide Rwanda resulted into a whole variety of different mechanisms being used to address the crimes. There was the aforementioned International Criminal Tribunal for Rwanda to prosecute the main and top level perpetrators of the genocide; there were the domestic courts of Rwanda to address the perpetrators one level below; and then there were traditional courts, called gacaca, to hold accountable the low-level perpetrators at the village level. Here a group of villagers without legal education would hear both the accused and the other members of the local community before either acquitting or sentencing the accused to community work or time in prison. Altogether more than one million Rwandans were processed through the gacaca system. Some observers consider this a valuable and meaningful recycling of a traditional justice mechanism; others, especially international human rights organisations, were rather critical, as gacaca did not live up to universal human rights standards, as for example the accused were not provided with defence lawyers. Also the victims of the genocide were divided; some would have preferred proper trials leading to serious prison sentences.

8. Transitional justice

Today all situations of genocide and mass atrocities raise the question of how crimes of the past can be addressed to achieve some form of justice, compensate victims and build a better future. Such efforts — whether trials, traditional forms of justice or truth and reconciliation commissions — belong to a field of research called transitional justice. The overall lesson from the Rwandan experience is that there is no one-size-fits-all solution to transitional justice situations — for each case of massive human rights violations, including genocide, the relevant society and the international community has to consider various factors in designing the appropriate response to the situation at hand. Punishment is what the Genocide Convention prescribes; punishment is what the victims may yearn for, but it might well be that punishment is only part of the answer when searching for truth, justice and reconciliation.

9. To prevent the crime of genocide

In addition to the duty to punish, the UN Genocide Convention stipulates one other obligation for all its member states: the duty to prevent genocide. The dual focus is already evident in the official title of the genocide treaty: the UN Convention on the Prevention and Punishment of the Crime of Genocide. There is also a substantial link between the two duties. Conflict researchers have shown that impunity — the lack of accountability for gross human rights violations — is one of the key factors facilitating the creation of a genocidal mentality. Conversely, if there is a credible threat of punishment, the potential perpetrator may reconsider whether to engage in a genocidal campaign. There is disagreement in the scholarly literature regarding how effective punishment as deterrence actually can be. Some writers suggest that a low-level perpetrator in the midst of a war might not respond to the vague threat of future prosecutions, but carry on with his orders. Concerning high-level perpetrators, sceptics put forward a different argument questioning the link between punishment and prosecutions. In this regard the question is not so much whether the threat of punishment can have any effect on the perpetrator or not — but rather whether this effect is detrimental to the solution of the conflict or the ending of the genocide. Some scholars argue that high-level perpetrators will continue with their crimes, as they have no incentive to enter into serious peace talks — if all that waits for them is a plane bringing them to the International Criminal Court in The Hague. Thus the threat of punishment could have unintended consequences and prolong the suffering of the victims. Other writers respond that eventually this configuration will work to strengthen the preventative effect of punishment, as in the future, once some high-level perpetrators indeed have been put in prison, political and military leaders will take the threat of an ICC indictment into their considerations *before* ordering massive human rights violations. This effect is undermined if perpetrators are offered an amnesty instead of continuing through the legal proceedings — not to speak of the victims' hunger for justice.

9.1 The duty to prevent genocide

The duty to prevent genocide itself is not spelt out in much detail in the UN Convention. Article 8 contains a weak reminder that treaty states can refer matters concerning genocide to the appropriate organs of the United Nations — but this is of course an option open to all UN member states even without their becoming a member of the genocide treaty. The most important provision in regard to prevention is indeed Article 1 of the Convention, according to which member states 'undertake to prevent' genocide. Since the aforementioned judgement of the International Court of Justice in the case between Bosnia and Serbia in 2007, it is clear that this brief statement actually entails a legal — not just a moral or political — duty to prevent genocide. The judges explained how this duty was to be effected. First of all it did not depend on whether a crisis was labelled genocide or not — a matter that often occupies much of the public debate, as shown most recently in the case of Darfur. Rather the duty to prevent genocide makes it necessary to act before one can determine that genocide has been committed, as that is the very idea of prevention. Therefore the duty to prevent is activated as soon as there is a serious threat of genocide. All member states of the UN Convention have to employ all means available to them in accordance with international law to prevent the situation from escalating into genocide. The closer a state is tied geographically, politically and economically to the state where genocide is about to be committed, the more comprehensive the duty to prevent genocide becomes. This was also what the Court pointed out vis-à-vis Serbia, indicating the strong ties Serbia had to the Bosnian Serbs in Bosnia and Herzegovina. The Court did not address the very controversial question under international law of whether states, even without a green light from the UN Security Council (the UN organ that is responsible for international peace and security) can send troops into a third state — without that state's consent — to prevent an impeding or stop an ongoing genocide. The Court did not refer to such humanitarian interventions, so the debate on whether, for example, the United States or NATO member states have the right or in fact are under an obligation to prevent the next Rwanda. The Court did, however, leave no doubt that all member states of the UN Genocide Convention are under a legal obligation to prevent genocide and prevention, of course, can come in many ways short of an armed intervention, including political and economic pressure.

One of the weak spots of this finding may be that there is no organ under the genocide treaty that can lobby states to meet this duty and later sanction them, if necessary, for non-compliance. It would take a new case before the International Court of Justice, with one state investing political will and courage in bringing another state to the Court, before the duty to prevent genocide would see legal enforcement. Another challenge to effective genocide prevention is that it took 14 years from when Bosnia and Herzegovina instituted proceedings against Serbia until the Court rendered its final judgement on the duty to prevent genocide.

9.2 'Responsibility to protect'

In light of these challenges, many observers place more hope on a parallel development at the United Nations. The new buzzword regarding genocide prevention is 'responsibility to protect' or in short 'R2P'. In 2005, on the 60th anniversary of the United Nations, a summit of all state leaders proclaimed in a General Assembly resolution that each state has a responsibility to protect its population from war crimes, crimes against humanity, ethnic cleansing and genocide. On a second level, the international community of states has a responsibility to assist states in exercising R2P by means of capacity building and other means of aid. If a state manifestly fails its responsibility to protect its population, this responsibility passes on to the international

community, which has the responsibility to respond to the crisis through the United Nations 161
and more specifically the UN Security Council. In a way, R2P did not add much to the existing
landscape of genocide prevention and certainly no new legal obligations, as General Assembly
resolutions are not legally binding — and yet, the introduction of R2P clearly has the potential
to strengthen genocide prevention.

First of all, there is a new commitment from all UN member states to prevent the committing
of large-scale atrocities and to respond to all the crimes listed in the definition of R2P, including
genocide. Secondly, there is conceptual progress, as sovereignty is no longer accepted as the
big stumbling block to genocide prevention. Sovereignty has been traditionally understood by
many as not interfering with the internal affairs of a given state; R2P redefined sovereignty
as a two-sided coin, which protected the sovereign state from outside intervention, but also
entailed certain responsibilities so that a state could not invoke its sovereignty to shield itself
from international scrutiny in the event of massive human rights violations being committed.
As with genocide prevention, it is crucial to recall that responsibility to protect also has a much
broader agenda than just armed intervention.

Since its introduction at the United Nations in 2005, R2P has scored mixed results. On the
positive side it has found its way into a number of Security Council resolutions and also started
to impact the mandates of UN peacekeeping operations. In addition, it has been the topic of
annual and substantial debates in the UN General Assembly, pushing forward the discussion on
how to implement R2P. For that purpose, the UN has also established an office headed by two
high-level officials to advise the UN Secretary General on both genocide prevention and R2P. On
the negative side, and not so surprisingly perhaps, it has shown that R2P is not immune against
misuse. It was, for example, invoked unilaterally by Russia — and not through the United Nations — during the conflict with Georgia in 2008. It also is dependent on the political goodwill
of states, as its mere invocation (as for example with regard to the Darfur crisis) does not
suffice to prevent or even stop mass atrocities. A new chapter in the history of R2P was written
by the recent UN-authorised NATO intervention in Libya during the spring of 2011, as this initially
seemed to be a successful R2P operation to prevent massive crimes being committed in the
Libyan town of Benghazi. Eventually, however, the NATO operation also involved giving strong
support to the Libyan rebels and thus caused widespread international criticism. Only time will
show whether Libya was the first of a series of successful R2P operations or whether now, more
than ever, sceptics view R2P as no more than a tool for Western states to impose their political
goals.

Major judgements concerning the crime of genocide

Case Concerning the Application of the Convention on the Prevention and Punishment of the Crime of Genocide, Bosnia and Herzegovina v. Serbia and Montenegro, International Court of Justice, 26 February 2007

This was the first substantive genocide judgement issued by the UN's highest judicial organ, the International Court of Justice (ICJ). The ICJ does not deal with the criminal accountability of individuals, but looks at the responsibility of states for violating international law. The Court held that Serbia did not commit genocide, but failed both to prevent the genocide committed by Bosnian Serbs at Srebrenica in July 1995 and to punish the perpetrators of this genocide.

Headquarters of the United Nations in New York with the flags of participating nations
Source: United Nations

Prosecutor v. Akayesu, International Criminal Tribunal for Rwanda, 2 September 1998

This was the first conviction for the crime of genocide by an international tribunal since the drafting of the Genocide Convention. Apart from its historical significance the judgement also sets forth an in-depth study of the facts of the Rwandan genocide. Legally, the inclusion of sexual violence, more specifically of rape, into the catalogue of acts that can constitute genocide is of major importance.

Prosecutor v. Jelisic, International Criminal Tribunal for the former Yugoslavia, 14 December 1999 (Trial Chamber) and 5 July 2001 (Appeals Chamber)

In this case the ICTY Trial Chamber starting to explore further aspects of the legal definition of genocide. Questions such as whether a single perpetrator can commit genocide in a local community are addressed. Furthermore, the Trial Chamber and the Appeals Chamber agree that the crime of genocide requires a very specific form of intent that distinguishes genocide from other offences such as crimes against humanity.

Prosecutor v. Krstic, International Criminal Tribunal for the former Yugoslavia, 2 August 2001 and 19 April 2004

This case entails the first genocide conviction by an international tribunal in Europe. The Trial Chamber found General Krstic guilty of genocide as responsible for the killing of more than 7,000 male inhabitants of the Bosnian town of Srebrenica. The judgement provides for a comprehensive overview of the events and discusses a number of issues surrounding the legal definition of genocide, including the question of what is meant by destroying a protected group 'in part'.

Key figure

Raphael Lemkin (1900-1959)
In 1944, the Polish lawyer Raphael Lemkin created the actual term 'genocide', joining the Greek word 'genos' (race, nation or tribe) and the Latin suffix 'cide' (from 'caedere', to kill). He introduced the concept of genocide in his book *Axis Rule in Occupied Europe*.

Glossary

The Nuremberg Trial	In 1945 and 1946 the triumphant allied forces installed the International Military Tribunal at the German city of Nuremberg. Here, some of the most important captured Nazi suspects were tried and in most cases convicted.
United Nations	International organization. Representatives of 50 countries signed on 26 June 1945 the United Nations Charter. The United Nations officially came into existence on 24 October 1945.
ICJ	The International Court of Justice. This court is the highest judicial organ of the United Nations and situated in The Hague, the Netherlands.
ICC	The International Criminal Court. A permanent and universal institution to prosecute international crimes, situated in The Hague, the Netherlands.
ICTR	The International Criminal Tribunal for Rwanda, a UN body to prosecute those with the greatest responsibility for the Rwandan genocide, situated in Arusha, Tanzania.
ICTY	The International Criminal Tribunal for the former Yugoslavia, a UN body to hold those accountable that were deemed responsible for the massive human rights violations during the then ongoing conflict in the former Yugoslavia, situated in The Hague, the Netherlands.
UN Security Council	Key organ of the UN, charged with the maintenance of international peace and security. 15 members — five permanent (United States, China, Russia, United Kingdom and France) and 10 non-permanent elected for two years according to regional groupings from the General Assembly. The Council established the ICTR and ICTY and can refer cases of alleged international crimes to the ICC.

ECCC	The Extraordinary Chambers in the Courts of Cambodia, the ECCC is not a purely international, independent organization, but placed within the domestic system and in part also staffed by nationals of the relevant state.
Genocidaires	French, 'those who commit genocide', referring to those guilty of genocidal acts during the Rwandan genocide in 1994.
UN Convention on the Prevention and Punishment of the Crime of Genocide	International treaty from 1948 with currently 142 member states. In force since 1951. In addition to the duty to punish, the UN Genocide Convention stipulates one other obligation for all its member states: the duty to prevent genocide.
R2P	Having failed in Rwanda and at Srebrenica, the international community agreed in 2005 that there is a 'responsibility to protect' (R2P). R2P is a political commitment, not a legally binding norm. According to R2P each state has to protect its population against genocide, crimes against humanity, war crimes and 'ethnic cleansing'. Second, the international community should assist states in this task. Third, if a state manifestly fails to live up to its responsibility, other states should exercise this responsibility through the United Nations. This includes peaceful means, but ultimately also the authorization of armed force as in NATO's operation in Libya in 2011.

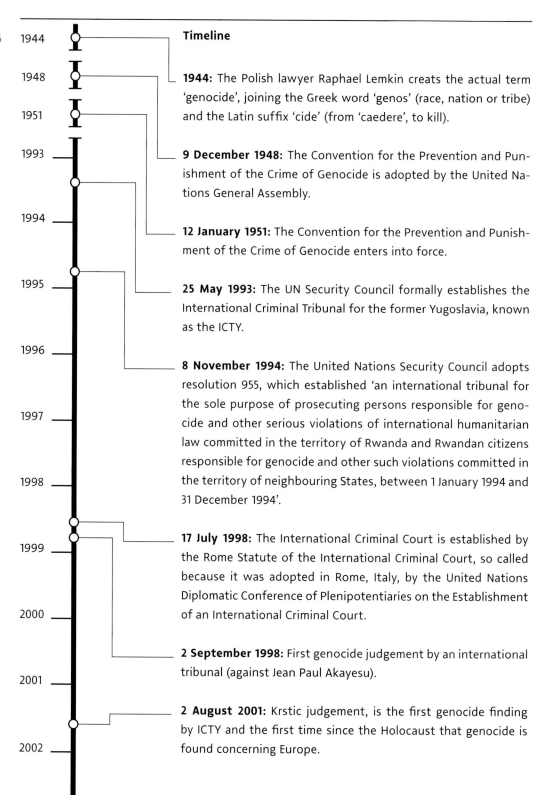

Timeline

1944

1948

1951

1993

1994

1995

1996

1997

1998

1999

2000

2001

2002

1944: The Polish lawyer Raphael Lemkin creats the actual term 'genocide', joining the Greek word 'genos' (race, nation or tribe) and the Latin suffix 'cide' (from 'caedere', to kill).

9 December 1948: The Convention for the Prevention and Punishment of the Crime of Genocide is adopted by the United Nations General Assembly.

12 January 1951: The Convention for the Prevention and Punishment of the Crime of Genocide enters into force.

25 May 1993: The UN Security Council formally establishes the International Criminal Tribunal for the former Yugoslavia, known as the ICTY.

8 November 1994: The United Nations Security Council adopts resolution 955, which established 'an international tribunal for the sole purpose of prosecuting persons responsible for genocide and other serious violations of international humanitarian law committed in the territory of Rwanda and Rwandan citizens responsible for genocide and other such violations committed in the territory of neighbouring States, between 1 January 1994 and 31 December 1994'.

17 July 1998: The International Criminal Court is established by the Rome Statute of the International Criminal Court, so called because it was adopted in Rome, Italy, by the United Nations Diplomatic Conference of Plenipotentiaries on the Establishment of an International Criminal Court.

2 September 1998: First genocide judgement by an international tribunal (against Jean Paul Akayesu).

2 August 2001: Krstic judgement, is the first genocide finding by ICTY and the first time since the Holocaust that genocide is found concerning Europe.

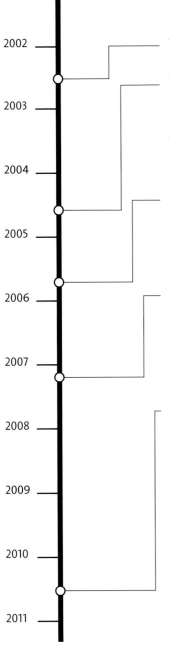

1 July 2002: The ICC Statute comes into force.

12 July 2004: Secretary-General Kofi Annan informs the United Nations Security Council that he has chosen Juan E. Méndez, a human rights advocate, lawyer and former political prisoner from Argentina, as his first Special Adviser on the Prevention of Genocide.

September 2005: At the United Nations World Summit, all Member States formally accept the responsibility of each State to protect its population from genocide, war crimes, ethnic cleansing and crimes against humanity.

26 February 2007: The International Court of Justice (ICJ) delivers its judgment in the case 'Application of the convention on the prevention and punishment of the crime of genocide, (Bosnia Herzegovina v. Serbia and Montenegro). It confirms the ICTY case-law in that the Srebrenica massacre was genocide.

12 July 2010: The International Criminal Court (ICC) issues an arrest warrant for President Omar al-Bashir of Sudan for genocide committed in Darfur. An earlier arrest warrant for al-Bashir was issued in March 2009 by the ICC for war crimes and crimes against humanity in Darfur.

References

The Holocaust, 1933-1941-1945

Bauer, Yehuda. and Nili Keren (1982). *A History of the Holocaust*. New York.

Bauer, Yehuda. (2001). *Rethinking the Holocaust*. New Haven.

Browning, Christopher. R. and Jürgen Mattäus (2004). *The Origins of the Final Solution: The Evolution of Nazi-Jewish Policy, September 1939-March 1942*. Lincoln.

Dwork, D. and R.J. van Pelt (2002). *Holocaust. A History*. New York.

Friedländer, Saul. (2007). *Nazi Germany and the Jews. The Years of Extermination 1939-1945*. New York.

Gerlach, Christian. (2010). *Extreme violent Societies. Mass Violence in the Twentieth-Century World*. Cambridge.

Hilberg, Raul. (2003). *The Destruction of the European Jews*. New Haven.

Kershaw, Ian. (2000). *Hitler 1936-1945, Nemesis*. New York.

Longerich, Peter. (2011). *Heinrich Himmler, A Life*. Oxford.

Pohl, Dieter. (2003). *Verfolgung und Massenmord in der NS-Zeit 1933-1945*. Darmstadt.

Online sources

http://www.armeensegenocide.info
http://www.armenian-genocide.org
http://www.genocide-museum.am

Bloxham, Donald (2005). *The Great Game of Genocide: Imperialism, Nationalism, and the Destruction of the Ottoman Armenians.* Oxford.

Gingeras, Ryan (2009). *Sorrowful Shores: Violence, Ethnicity, and the End of the Ottoman Empire, 1912-1923.* Oxford.

Göçek, Fatma Müge, Norman Naimark and Ronald Grigor Suny (eds.) (2011). *A Question of Genocide: Armenians and Turks at the End of the Ottoman Empire.* New York.

Gust, Wolfgang (ed.) (2005). *Der Völkermord an den Armeniern 1915/16: Dokumente aus dem Politischen Archiv des deutschen Auswärtigen Amts.* Hamburg.

Kévorkian, Raymond H. (2011). *The Armenian Genocide: A Complete History.* London.

Üngör, Uğur Ümit (2011). *The Making of Modern Turkey: Nation and State in Eastern Anatolia, 1913-1950.* Oxford.

Üngör, Uğur Ümit and Mehmet Polatel (2011). *Confiscation and Destruction: The Young Turk Seizure of Armenian Property.* London.

Extra material

For reports by and interviews with eyewitnesses to the genocide, see:
http://www.chgs.umn.edu/histories/turkisharmenian/eyewitness.html
http://www.theforgotten.org
http://www.twentyvoices.com

Miller, Donald E. and Lorne Touryan-Miller (1993). *Survivors: An Oral History of the Armenian Genocide.* Berkeley, CA: University of California Press.

Totten, Samuel, William S. Parsons and Israel W. Charny (eds.) (1997). *Century of Genocide: Eyewitness Accounts and Critical Views*, New York. pp. 53-92

Online sources

http://www.cambodiatribunal.org
http://www.eccc.gov.kh/en
http://www.yale.edu/cgp

Boua, Chanthou (1991). 'Genocide of a Religious Group: Pol Pot and Cambodia's Buddhist Monks', pp. 227-40. In: P.T. Bushnell, V. Schlapentokh, C. Vanderpool and J. Sundram (eds.) *State-Organized Terror: The Case of Violent Internal Repression*. Boulder, CO.

Boua, Chanthou, David P. Chandler and Ben Kiernan (eds.) (1988). *Pol Pot Plans the Future: Confidential Leadership Documents from Democratic Kampuchea, 1976-77*. New Haven, CT: Yale Council on Southeast Asia Studies.

Burr, W. and M.L. Evans (eds.) (2001). 'Text of Ford-Kissinger-Suharto Discussion, U.S. Embassy Jakarta Telegram 1579 to Secretary State, December 6, 1975'. In: *East Timor Revisited: Ford, Kissinger and the Indonesian Invasion, 1975-76*. Washington: National Security Archive.

Chandler, David P. (1991). *The Tragedy of Cambodian History*. New Haven, CT.

Jackson, Karl (ed.) (1989). *Cambodia 1975-1978: Rendezvous with Death*. Princeton, N.J.

Kiernan, Ben (1985). *How Pol Pot Came to Power: A History of Communism in Kampuchea, 1930-1975*. London.

Kiernan, Ben (1986). *Cambodia: Eastern Zone Massacres*. New York: Columbia University, Centre for the Study of Human Rights, Documentation Series No. 1.

Kiernan, Ben (1988). 'Orphans of Genocide: The Cham Muslims of Kampuchea under Pol Pot'. In: *Bulletin of Concerned Asian Scholars*, 20(4): 2-33.

Kiernan, Ben (1989). 'Blue Scarf/Yellow Star: A Lesson in Genocide'. In: *Boston Globe*, February 27, p. 13.

Kiernan, Ben (1990). 'The Survival of Cambodia's Ethnic Minorities'. *Cultural Survival*, 14(3): 64-66.

Kiernan, Ben (1991). 'Deferring Peace in Cambodia: Regional Rapprochement, Superpower Obstruction', pp. 59-82. In: George W. Breslauer, Harry Kreisler, and Benjamin Ward (eds.) *Beyond the Cold War*. Berkeley: Institute of International Studies, University of California.

Kiernan, Ben (2002, second edition with new preface; 2008, third edition 2008). *The Pol Pot Regime: Race, Power and Genocide in Cambodia under the Khmer Rouge, 1975-1979*. New Haven, CT.

Kiernan, Ben (2008). *Genocide and Resistance in Southeast Asia: Documentation, Denial, and Justice in Cambodia and East Timor*. New Brunswick, NJ.

Kiernan, Ben (2009). 'The Cambodian Genocide 1975-1979'. In: Samuel Totten and William S. Parsons (eds.) *Century of Genocide: Critical Essays and Eyewitness Accounts*. New York, p. 368.

Leopold, Evelyn (1991). 'Western Nations Want Former Cambodian Leader to Leave Country'. September 22. *Reuters Cable*, UN (NYC).

Kiernan, Ben and Boua Chanthou (eds.) (1982). *Peasants and Politics in Kampuchea, 1942-1981*. London.

Migozzi, Jacques (1973). *Cambodge: faits et problémes de population*. Paris: Centre National de la Recherche Scientifique.

Pol Pot (1978). *Interview of Comrade Pol Pot… to the Delegation of Yugoslav Journalists in Visit to Democratic Kampuchea. March 23*. Phnom Penh: Democratic Kampuchea, Ministry of Foreign Affairs.

Shawcross, William (1979). *Sideshow: Kissinger, Nixon and the Destruction of Cambodia*. New York.

Shenon, Philip (1991). 'Cambodian Factions Sign Peace Pact'. October 24, *New York Times*, p. A16.

Vickery, Michael (1984). *Cambodia 1975-1982*. Boston.

Online sources

http://blogs.ushmm.org/WorldIsWitness/region/C40/
http://www.hrw.org/en/reports/1999/03/01/leave-none-tell-story
http://www.kigalimemorialcentre.org
http://www.yale.edu/gsp/rwanda/

Dallaire, Roméo (2004). *Shake Hands with the Devil*. Toronto.

Gourevitch, Philip (1998). *We Wish to Inform You That Tomorrow We Will be Killed With Our Families: Stories from Rwanda*. New York.

Hatzfield, Jean (2006). *Machete Season: The killers in Rwanda speak*. London.

Power, Samantha (2003). *A Problem from Hell: America and the Age of Genocide*. New York.

Banac, Ivo (1994). *The National Question in Yugoslavia. Origins, History, Politics*. (1984) Ithaca/London.

Cigar, Norman (1995). *Genocide in Bosnia. The Policy of 'Ethnic Cleansing'*. College Station.

Glenny, Misha (1993). *The Fall of Yugoslavia. The Third Balkan War*. New edition. Harmondsworth.

Glenny, Misha (1999). *The Balkans, 1804-1999. Nationalism, War, and the Great Powers*. London.

Kennan, George F. 'The Balkan Crisis: 1913 and 1993', *New York Review of Books*. (15.07.93)

Kinross, Lord (1977). *The Ottoman Centuries. The Rise and Fall of the Turkish Empire*. New York.

Mennecke, Martin and Eric Markusen (2003). 'The International Criminal Tribunal for the Former Yugoslavia and the Crime of Genocide'. In: Steven L.B. Jensen (ed.) *Genocide: Cases, Comparisons and Contemporary Debates*. Copenhagen: The Danish Center for Holocaust and Genocide Studies.

Petersen, Roger D. (2002). *Understanding Ethnic Violence. Fear, Hatred, and Resentment in Twentieth-Century Eastern Europe*. Cambridge.

Polonsky, Anthony (1975). *The Little Dictators. The History of Eastern Europe since 1918*. London.

Power, Samantha (2002). *A Problem from Hell. America and the Age of Genocide*. New York.

Silber, Laura en Allan Little (1995). *The Death of Yugoslavia*. Harmondsworth.

Skocpol, Theda (1979). *States and Social Revolutions*. Cambridge.

Thompson, Mark (1994). *Forging War: The Media in Serbia, Croatia and Bosnia-Herzegovina*. Washington.

Zimmermann, Warren. 'The Captive Mind', *New York Review of Books*. (02.02.95)

Online sources

http://ictj.org/
http://iwpr.net/
http://www.responsibilitytoprotect.org
http://www.un.org/en/preventgenocide/adviser/index.shtml
http://www.unhchr.ch/html/menu3/b/p_genoci.htm
http://www.unhchr.ch/html/menu3/b/treaty1gen.htm
http://untreaty.un.org/cod/avl/ha/cppcg/cppcg.html

Ratner, Steven R., Jason S. Abrams and James L. Bischoff (2009). *Accountability for Human Rights Atrocities in International Law – Beyond the Nuremberg Legacy.* 3rd edition. Oxford.
Schabas, William A. (2009). *Genocide in International Law – The Crime of Crimes.* 2nd edition. Cambridge
Zahar, Alexander and Göran Sluiter (2008). *International Criminal Law – A Critical Introduction.* Oxford.

Maria van Haperen (b. 1960) studied at Radboud University Nijmegen. She is a historian, teacher and publicist. Since 2005 she has worked as an education specialist for the NIOD Institute for War, Holocaust and Genocide Studies. She also conceived, wrote and edited the secondary school history teaching methods Sfinx and Feniks. She worked as an editor for the *Historisch Nieuwsblad* and Kleio and was awarded the Hartog Beem Prize.

Wichert ten Have (b. 1944) is a historian and director of Holocaust and Genocide Studies at the NIOD Institute for War, Holocaust and Genocide Studies. In 1995, he was awarded his PhD for research into the Nederlandsche Unie, a political movement that called for cooperation with the Nazis during the German occupation of the Netherlands. As a lecturer, he is also associated with the Master's programme in Holocaust and Genocide Studies at the University of Amsterdam.

Benedict F. Kiernan (b. 1953) is Whitney Griswold Professor of History, Professor of International and Area Studies and director of the Genocide Studies Program. He was founding Director of the Cambodian Genocide Program (1994-1999) and Convener of the Yale East Timor Project (2000-2002). He is the author of *Blood and Soil: A World History of Genocide and Extermination from Sparta to Darfur* (2007), which won several prizes, such as the gold medal for the best book in History awarded by the Independent Publishers association.

Martin Mennecke (b. 1973) is an Assistant Professor of International Law at the University of Copenhagen, Denmark, and a visiting lecturer at the University of Greenland in Nuuk, Greenland. He holds an LLM in public international law from the University of Edinburgh and a PhD in international criminal law from the University of Frankfurt, Germany. His current research interests include the International Criminal Court, the responsibility to protect and the role of international law in the Arctic. Mennecke is a member of the Danish delegations to the Assembly of State Parties to the International Criminal Court and the International Whaling Commission. He participates as academic adviser in meetings at the United Nations and the European Union. He has previously been a member of the Danish delegation to the International Task Force on Holocaust Education, Research and Remembrance and was the founding co-chairperson of the sub-committee on the Holocaust and other genocides in the Task Force Education Working Group.

Uğur Ümit Üngör (b. 1980) obtained his PhD *cum laude* at the University of Amsterdam in 2009. He was connected to the Centre for Holocaust and Genocide Studies (2005-2008), and the universities of Sheffield (2008-2009) and Dublin (2009-2010). He is currently an assistant professor of History at Utrecht University and a researcher at the NIOD Institute for War, Holocaust and Genocide Studies, specialising in the historical sociology of mass violence. His most recent publications are *The Making of Modern Turkey: Nation and State in Eastern Anatolia, 1913-1950* (2011), and *Confiscation and Destruction: The Young Turk Seizure of Armenian Property* (2011).

Ton Zwaan (b. 1946) studied social sciences at the University of Amsterdam. He has worked at Radboud University Nijmegen as a researcher for the Institute of Cultural and Social Anthropology, at the University of Amsterdam as a member of the Sociology and History department and at the Open University as a member of the Faculty of Cultural Sciences. Until 2011 he was assistant professor at the Anthropology and Sociology Department of the University of Amsterdam and a member of the academic staff at the NIOD Institute for War, Holocaust and Genocide Studies. His publications include *Civilisering en decivilisering* [Civilising and decivilising] (2001) and *Genocide en de crisis van Joegoslavië 1985-2005* [Genocide and the crisis of Yugoslavia 1985-2005] (2005).